Software Change Management: Case Studies and Practical Advice

Donald J. Reifer

PUBLISHED BY
Microsoft Press
A Division of Microsoft Corporation
One Microsoft Way
Redmond, Washington 98052-6399

Library of Congress Control Number: 2011942372
ISBN: 978-0-7356-6475-3

Printed and bound in the United States of America.

First Printing

Microsoft Press books are available through booksellers and distributors worldwide. If you need support related to this book, email Microsoft Press Book Support at mspinput@microsoft.com. Please tell us what you think of this book at *http://www.microsoft.com/learning/booksurvey.*

Acquisitions Editor: Devon Musgrave
Developmental Editor: Devon Musgrave
Project Editor: Valerie Woolley
Editorial Production: Curtis Philips, Publishing.com
Copyeditor: Roger LeBlanc
Indexer: Lucie Haskins
Cover: Twist Creative • Seattle

Dedicated to those serving as agents of change,
I applaud you.

Contents at a Glance

Contents

Chapter 12 Making an Impact 141

What do you think of this book? We want to hear from you!

Microsoft is interested in hearing your feedback so we can continually improve our books and learning resources for you. To participate in a brief online survey, please visit:

microsoft.com/learning/booksurvey

Foreword

When you're making decisions about addressing upcoming opportunities and challenges, it is a good practice to do an Analysis of Alternatives. And it is also a good practice to include "Don't change what you're currently doing" as one of the alternatives. In many cases, this can be the best alternative, as reflected in such maxims as "If it ain't broke, don't fix it," "Plan the flight and fly the plan," and "Hold steady on the course."

But there are more and more situations in which "Don't change" is a very risky alternative. A good set of examples is the analysis in Eberhardt Rechtin's book, *Systems Architecting of Organizations: Why Eagles Can't Swim."* Rechtin explains why on six successive satellite system replacement competitions, the more experienced incumbents just did some modifications of their previous winning designs and lost to more innovative competitors. In order to remain competitive in a world of increasing change velocity, you'll want to consider alternatives to "Don't change," and to provide evidence in your Analysis of Alternatives to opponents of change when "Don't change" is not a good idea.

Is the velocity of change all that rapid? In 2006, I published a paper* that tried to anticipate future trends and to prepare organizations for accommodating them. By 2011, I found that I had not covered several trends that turned out to be further game-changers for organizations. Most of them were software-intensive: service-oriented cloud computing; social networking technologies; mega-sensor-intensive smart systems; multicore chips requiring software parallelization; and search and mining of ultra-large data aggregations. And the pace of change continues to accelerate, not just in technology, but also in competition and the marketplace. Not only is it important to monitor these changes, but it's at least as important to master the art of making successful organizational change.

This is what makes Don Reifer's book particularly timely and helpful. Getting an organization to change requires getting many stakeholders and suborganizations—who often won't want to change or would like to manipulate the change to increase their power base—to come together, to agree on a mutually satisfactory change strategy, and to contribute their key resources to making the change successful.

Besides Don's technical contributions to such areas as cyber security, cost estimation, business case analysis, software project management, and software maintenance, he has been an effective change agent as a consultant to a remarkably wide variety of

---

* B. Boehm, "Some Future Trends and Implications for Systems and Software Engineering Processes," *Systems Engineering,* Wiley Periodicals, Inc., Volume 9, Issue 1, 2006, pp. 1-19

organizations. These include large and small financial, telecommunications, aerospace, software tools, gaming, and Internet startup companies, and public service organizations. In the book, he provides case studies drawn from these various sectors that illustrate how they have dealt with the need for change to address opportunities or problems at a project, department, business area, or enterprise level.

Along the way, the generally successful case studies illustrate pitfalls to avoid, such as trying to change things outside your span of control, neglecting to provide incentives for change to success-critical stakeholders or leaving them out of the planning process, trying to change too many things in one step, and failing to provide a sound business case for a change initiative.

The diversity of the case studies means that not all of them will be relevant to everyone's situation, but that most people will find some of them to be highly relevant. And the diversity is brought together in the final chapter, which includes ten change management secrets of success; a dozen change management lessons learned; ten useful tools in change management; and summaries of change management critical success factors in dealing with senior managers and in dealing with the workers who will implement the changes. As a bottom line, this book can be very valuable in helping you cope with the increasing pace of change that you'll encounter during your career.

Barry Boehm
September 2011

The phrase "software process improvement" has become a catchphrase for the software industry and occurs hundreds of times in monthly journal articles and also in scores of books. But what does the phrase really mean and how do the concepts get applied in the real world? Don Reifer has been studying software in major companies for many years and has assisted many in improving software development methods and practices.

Process improvement is closely linked to change management. Change in corporations is sometimes glacial and often resisted strongly. Don's book includes some interesting factual information, and also procedural information, about introducing both structural changes and organizational changes that do not disrupt ongoing operations.

At the level of individual projects, change control is also a critical factor. In fact, from my observations while working as an expert witness in software litigation, the two main sources of lawsuits are poor quality control and poor change control.

The measured rate at which software projects change is between 1 and 2 percent per calendar month. For large systems with schedules in the 36 to 48 month range, more than 25 percent of the features that are present at delivery were not there when the requirements were first defined. They came in later due to either incomplete requirements gathering or external business changes that were not predictable.

Don's new book is not a theoretical treatise on change management and software process improvement, but rather it's a series of a dozen empirical case studies from both companies and government groups. The book also covers improvements in both development and maintenance operations.

Software change management and process improvement involve more than mere acquisition of a few tools that support specific methods such as Agile or the Team Software Process. Rather, the issues addressed include a full spectrum of organization topics, methodological topics, tools, and the measurement and reporting of improvement results. In fact, the measurement and reporting of results has been the Achilles heel of many process improvement attempts. The organizations may get better, but if they don't measure the improvements and the costs needed to achieve the improvements then fairly soon top executives will cut off the funding.

Yet another area that needs attention during process improvement activities is the sociological areas of relationships between the information technology (IT) group and its clients, and between the various components of the information technology organization itself.

In many IT shops, the IT world and the client world tend to be adversarial rather than collegial. The adversarial relationships are even worse inside IT groups themselves.

There is often friction between the test community and the development groups, between the maintenance teams and the development teams, and between quality assurance and development teams.

Ordinary corporate politics also play a role, and sometimes projects are canceled because managers don't like each other and refuse to cooperate.

The ten case studies and the shorter anecdotes in Don's book also include some subjects not normally covered in the process literature, such as enabling an academic institute to form a better partnership with information technology companies.

The book provides a very valuable source of empirical data taken from real organizations. The book shows in a step-by-step fashion what the original conditions were, and then the changes that were introduced to improve the initial conditions. These are not trivial changes in small organizations; they are major long-term changes in large and complex organizations.

In general, Don's observations are congruent with my own research on change control and software process improvement. The gist of my findings and the gist of Don's findings are similar:

- Project management is frequently a bottleneck and must be included in all improvements.

- Quality needs to improve first; otherwise, being faster generates more bugs.

- Software defect prevention often needs improvement.

- Pre-test inspections and static analysis often need to be added to quality methods.

- The front end of software projects in requirement and design are often weak links.

- Training and education of all personnel, including management, should be continuous.

- Organization structures are important aspects of process improvements.

- Special care is needed in handling project office, test groups, quality assurance, and other specialist organizations.

- Change control, requirements creep, and deferred features also need to be evaluated.

- Measurement and results are important from day 1 and should become permanent fixtures.

- Executive support is needed, and it requires positive return on investment (ROI) results.

- Processes need to encompass total costs of ownership (TCO).

- Processes need to encompass package acquisition as well as internal development.

- Processes need to encompass contracts and outsourcing as well as internal development.

- Once process improvements occur, new personnel and new managers need to be trained in what the best practices are to ensure continuity.

- The goals of change control and process improvements are closer and more harmonious alignment between business operations and software activities.

Overall, Don's book provides a solid and valuable contribution to the literature on change management and software process improvement methods. It is a book with a very broad focus, and it covers a wide range of topics. This is what the industry needs—not a narrow view of a single method that is claimed to be a panacea.

As Fred Brooks pointed out years ago in *The Mythical Man-Month*, there is no "silver bullet." To get better in software, a wide variety of organizational, social, and technical issues must be addressed in a rational sequence. Don's book adds to this concept and offers a variety of interesting case studies from many organizations.

Capers Jones
President, Capers Jones & Associates LLC
August 2011

Introduction

This book presents ten case studies that revolve around how to manage change in industrial, governmental, and academic settings. Each case was selected to communicate lessons learned that the reader can use to address typical issues that occur during the process of change. Context-sensitive knowledge about how others managed change within these settings is communicated by describing what others did when faced with adversity.

Who Should Read This Book

This book was written to equip those making and managing changes in software organizations with the processes, techniques, and tools that they need to be successful. If you are involved in change initiatives, this book is for you because it points out what the typical issues are that you will face and how others in similar situations have dealt with them.

This book is targeted for consumption by a broad range of readers, from executives to those software engineers who want to pursue change initiatives aimed at getting the job of software development and maintenance done quicker, smarter, and better. Professors will also find this text helpful in communicating the fundamentals associated with instituting and managing change in organizations. Entrepreneurs and business people might want to take advantage of concepts included within the case studies that describe how to facilitate making the changes necessary to transition products to market quicker. Researchers might find the text useful in structuring how they package their new research developments for eventual commercialization.

Assumptions

This book expects that you have at least a basic understanding of underlying software engineering and management fundamentals that set the context for the changes described within the case studies. If you need refresher materials in these topics, you might consider reading Steve McConnell's *Code Complete,* Second Edition (Microsoft Press, 2004), Roger Pressman's *Software Engineering: A Practitioner's Approach,* Seventh Edition (McGraw-Hill, 2009), and Donald Reifer's *Software Management,* Seventh Edition (Wiley/IEEE Computer Society, 2006).

Who Should Not Read This Book

While this book might be interesting reading for entry-level software engineers, such readers need to be warned that the book presents only the background information needed to understand the management structure, industrial practices, implementation issues, and underlying technology for each of the case studies covered. Because the knowledge needed to fully understand the issues more deeply can take years to learn for the uninitiated, these readers and others from non-software backgrounds are warned that some of the discussions on how to resolve problems may be beyond their capacity to fully understand.

Organization of This Book

This book is organized around ten case studies. Chapter 1, "Getting Started," presents some background and context materials for these cases, while Chapter 12, "Making an Impact," provides a summary of lessons learned. The other ten chapters focus on learning experiences presented as case studies that range from making needed organizational changes in a large Information Technology (IT) shop to addressing adoption of Agile methods in a smaller, high technology organization. While based on real-world experiences, all of the cases represent fictitious examples developed to highlight different change management messages. Each of these ten cases is trying to communicate that change is hard and no matter what you do to facilitate the transition to something new, people will resist it. In response, each case tries to highlight the change management principles you can use to make the change and get the job done, often over the objections of others who are more comfortable with the status quo.

Online Companion Content

For those using this text in software engineering courses, I have authored an Instructor's Manual. The purpose of the manual is to help the instructor organize discussions for each of the ten case studies presented in a systematic manner. The manual might also assist others reading the book to determine all of the messages that the cases are trying to communicate. It was fun to write and should be fun to read.

The Instructor's Manual can be downloaded from the following page:

http://go.microsoft.com/FWLink/?Linkid=233071

Acknowledgments

I would like to first thank my team of peer reviewers, including Bob Charette, Bob Epps, Dr. Ken Nidiffer, and Joan Weszka for their contributions. Their reviews looked at content and made sure the cases presented in the majority of the chapters made sense. I want to next thank Valerie Woolley and her Microsoft Press team for the wonderful job they did editing and preparing the final manuscript. They added a great deal of value by making sure the messages that I tried to communicate in the cases came through by polishing my presentation. Lastly, I would like to thank my family and wife, Carole, who persevered as I wrote this volume. She proofed the early versions of the manuscript and helped me organize my thoughts more coherently.

Errata & Book Support

We've made every effort to ensure the accuracy of this book and its companion content. Any errors that have been reported since this book was published are listed on our Microsoft Press site at oreilly.com:

http://go.microsoft.com/FWLink/?Linkid=233089

If you find an error that is not already listed, you can report it to us through the same page.

If you need additional support, email Microsoft Press Book Support at *mspinput@ microsoft.com*.

Please note that product support for Microsoft software is not offered through the addresses above.

We Want to Hear from You

At Microsoft Press, your satisfaction is our top priority, and your feedback our most valuable asset. Please tell us what you think of this book at:

http://www.microsoft.com/learning/booksurvey

The survey is short, and we read every one of your comments and ideas. Thanks in advance for your input!

Stay in Touch

Let's keep the conversation going! We're on Twitter: *http://twitter.com/MicrosoftPress*

CHAPTER 1

Getting Started

This book is about making needed changes within software organizations. As such, its focus is on helping you get rid of inefficiencies, waste, and incompetence that make completing a software development or maintenance project more difficult. It differs from other books on change you might read by presenting case studies instead of emphasizing either the fundamentals or processes involved in facilitating organizational change. By providing these examples, I hope to show you what to do and how to react in a variety of situations that might or might not be supportive of your change proposals. These situations mimic those you will find in real-world industrial and government settings. Although they encompass mostly software development projects, maintenance jobs are covered as well. So are large and small projects, where size is measured in terms of team size and organizational dynamics.

By reading this book, you'll discover what works and what does not when you're placed in different operational situations involving change. Issues abound when you propose or pursue options to minimize disruption and maximize organizational benefits but which require a great deal of change to accomplish that. Some of these issues are operational, while many others are managerial and psychological. If you find your organization is resistant to change for whatever reasons, you can consult the case studies, which illustrate techniques to use to break down these barriers. Resistance to change is natural in most operational settings, and the topic is covered extensively in this book. The major reason for this resistance is comfort—that is, people tend to be comfortable with the status quo.

For example, a number of cases show you how to sell an idea on how to improve productivity based on its merits. As options, you might want to try either introducing a new technology or optimizing some process to make it more efficient. The case studies show you how to scope and sell the proposal based on the benefits to the organization and how to manage the resulting project to achieve your goals.

You will also find this book useful when faced with issues that impede progress on such change proposals. Because I use issue-based and action-oriented cases, you get practical advice on how to overcome the barriers that pop up. For each case, I start by describing the organization, the team, and the operational environment in which they reside. This description sets the context for the case. Next, I address issues and alternatives before discussing the actions taken and the results. These discussions are aimed at providing you with insights into what happens when various options are pursued under similar circumstances. Be forewarned, though, that the results detailed might not work the same for you because you may be operating under different conditions—not all seemingly similar situations are, in reality, the same.[1] Finally, I end each case with pointers to resources (such as literature and web-based resources) if appropriate ones exist and are readily accessible via hypertext. These pointers provide you with additional help if you're pursuing like options within a similar context.

Goals and scope

My goal in writing this book is to help you understand how to increase your chances of success when proposing, justifying, and implementing software changes. Such changes can be to management, infrastructure, processes, product standards, organizational or team structures, platforms, methodology, and tooling or underlying technology. Any of these changes can be justified if they result in improvements, especially when there are compelling operational needs.

I hope to provide insights into change management using the framework illustrated in Figure 1-1. I review each element of the pyramid at the beginning of each of the ten case studies. Each of these elements is needed to gain an understanding because it focuses on an important aspect of the operating environment in which the case operates—for example, its organizational structure, the types of projects pursued, the product being developed, the processes being used to develop it, and the people who perform the work. Taken singly, each element paints a different view of the case. Taken together, they provide a comprehensive view of the environment.

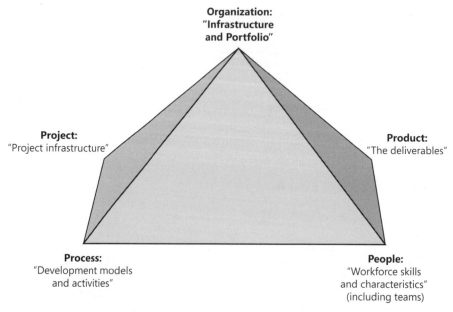

FIGURE 1-1 The operating environment pyramid.

Organization

The following aspects of organizations that might or might not develop software as their mainline products are described in the case studies. These aspects focus on the infrastructure that the enterprise establishes to manage its product portfolios and the organizational units it has established to develop them:

- Focus on accomplishment of business goals, both long-term and short-term
- Clear lines of communications and accountability
- Authority commensurate with responsibility
- Enlightened leadership (champions for justifiable change)
- Portfolio management and enterprise-wide processes

The organizational infrastructure is discussed in each of the cases to some degree because it directly influences outcomes involving change. Change is almost impossible if the enterprise does not support the pursuit of improvement initiatives.

Project

Projects are established in many organizations to provide dedicated management for product development and maintenance. Project management processes are used in such organizations to plan the project and to organize, obtain, and direct the resources needed to successfully accomplish the goals established for the project. Project managers should embrace the following resources, which will be discussed in the cases that involve projects:

- Proven project management processes
- Adequate time and resources to do the job
- Insightful measurement and control processes
- Responsible risk and opportunity management processes
- Teamwork, including working on Integrated Product Teams (IPTs) and a focus on getting the work done

Note that some enterprises do not use project management concepts. Instead, they dedicate the resources within a single organization to get the software job done. For example, an enterprise might develop software products and services using a product line rather than a project organizational structure. As you might expect, project aspects within such a context are omitted from the case studies used in this book.

Process

Processes are used at the organizational and project levels to structure the activities pursued and provide guidance for their orderly and disciplined completion. Process frameworks such as ISO/IEC 12207[2] and ISO/IEC 15288[3] and the Software Engineering Institute's (SEI) Capability Maturity Model Integration[4] (CMMI) provide structure for implementing a responsive systems/software process framework and improvement program. Processes such as these provide organizations with the following resources, which will be discussed in the case studies:

- Strong executive support for process improvement efforts

- Effective systems and software engineering processes and best practices

- Comprehensive maintenance and sustaining engineering processes and best practices

- Responsive product management (such as configuration management, distribution management, and quality assurance)

- Superior acquisition or supply chain management and licensing processes

Because of its importance, *process* is discussed in all of the cases. In addition to process frameworks, some of the cases discuss Agile methods[5] such as the Rational Unified Process[6] (RUP) and techniques such as the Team Software Process[7] (TSP).

Product

Organizational and project ventures are typically directed toward generating products and services that satisfy user requirements and, for commercial enterprises, make a profit. Intrinsic attributes such as the following are discussed in each case study because they can make or break the software product:

- Planned evolutionary paths and renewal cycles

- Traceability between requirements and product features

- Well-architected and well-engineered developments

- Superior craftsmanship and construction

- Demonstrable quality attributes (such as usable, reliable, and maintainable)

People

The wildcard in most software organizations and projects is people. Their skills, knowledge, and abilities often are the difference between success and failure of a development project. Their motivation and ability to work as members of a team can have a major influence on whether the job gets done right the first time. Because of the impact available personnel have on a project, each case provides a description of some of the following personnel characteristics:

- Highly skilled and motivated workforce

- Trained, efficient, and effective workers

- Experience in similar application domains

- Interdisciplinary and integrated product teams

- Ethics, accountability, and clear responsibility

Because of the potential impact of an organization's personnel policies (on attracting staff or the rate of turnover), I discuss practices used to recruit, reward (through promotions, salary increases, and bonuses), and retain skilled and able software personnel.

Change agents and their role

Many people involved in facilitating justifiable changes within software organizations are referred to as *change agents*. A change agent is a person who is directly or indirectly involved in change. This is not the person who sponsors, champions, proposes, or implements the change. Rather, the term refers to someone who has the skills, knowledge, and ability to provide others with the advice and guidance needed to make the proposed change a reality. Table 1-1 summarizes the typical roles of people involved in software change efforts.[8] The eight-step change process is summarized in Figure 1-2. As noted in the table, anyone can propose a change. However, lots of support is needed along with a team to implement the change effort. Sometimes a project has sufficient resources to propose and implement the change. Other times, the change has to be executed by an independent team because of either operational risks or resource limitations.

TABLE 1-1 Typical roles of people involved in the change process.

Role	Activities
Change Initiator (anyone in the organization)	■ Proposes a change based on need ■ Documents the change needed, and submits it using the established practice or process ■ Justifies the change, and acts as its proponent ■ Promotes the change until approved
Change Agent	■ Provides insight into the change process ■ Provides advice that addresses barriers, resolves issues, and generates results ■ Acts as an independent set of eyes and ears as the change process unfolds
Champion (a project pilot or other mid-level manager)	■ Promotes the change at the middle management level ■ Provides the resources to implement the change ■ Removes obstacles that are under his or her control ■ Addresses issues, and generates results

Role	Activities
Sponsor (an executive-level supporter)	■ Promotes the change at the senior management level ■ Provides executive support and coaching ■ Buffers the team against interference from above ■ Provides the budget, and protects it against pilfering
Opinion Leaders (technical leaders who are respected by their peers)	■ Makes the technical case for change (shows that it's the right thing to do) ■ Convinces others that the change makes sense ■ Takes charge of overseeing the work
Infrastructure Managers (process group leads or marketing personnel)	■ Adjusts the infrastructure to accommodate change ■ Promotes the change through actions and deeds ■ Promotes the change through infrastructure resources (such as newsletters, websites, and success stories)
Implementation Team	■ Implements the change ■ Verifies that the change does what it was supposed to do ■ Believes that the change is the right thing to do ■ Provides evidence that the change is beneficial and meets quantitative objectives, and if it does not, documents failure, declares success, and moves on

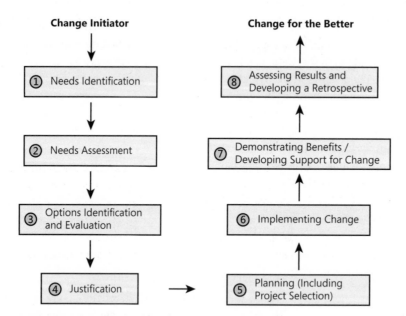

FIGURE 1-2 Organizational change implementation cycle.

The typical steps involved in the generalized organizational change process are illustrated in Figure 1-2 and briefly explained as follows:

1. **Needs Identification** The proposer has a good idea. That person identifies a desired change and then scopes and documents it.

2. **Needs Assessment**   The proposer verifies that the proposed change will result in positive results by conducting an impact assessment.

3. **Options Identification and Evaluation**   The proposer gathers more information about the feasible options (including doing nothing) associated with the change and why the change is needed.

4. **Justification**   The proposer develops a more detailed justification for the change in terms of dollars and cents and then submits a proposal to management for action.

5. **Planning (Including Project Selection)**   An implementation team and support group for the change is formed, and a detailed plan of action and milestones for implementation are developed by them for approval by management.

6. **Implementing Change**   The plan is approved by management and implemented by the team, who make mid-course corrections if needed as issues arise (delays, budget cuts, key personnel losses, resistance, and so forth) during execution.

7. **Demonstrating Benefits/Developing Support for Change**   The team demonstrates the benefits associated with the change and broadcasts their successes incrementally to solidify support. The philosophy that a sum of small successes yields a large success is adopted.

8. **Assessing Results and Developing a Retrospective**   The change is fully implemented, goals are achieved, measurements are recorded, and a retrospective[9] is written to document results.

Making a difference

There are many reasons for change in software organizations. Most revolve around the status quo. Organizations can get stagnant. This is especially damaging when they operate in an environment that is constantly changing. As business goals shift, so do the organizations, processes, people, and underlying technology (such as tools, methods, and management techniques) used to generate them. However, there needs to be either some compelling business or technical reason for change. Otherwise, why expend the resources to implement it? The ten most common reasons for organizational change I have observed are the following:

- **A crisis materializes**   A primary reason for change in many organizations is that some crisis occurs. For example, one of the key suppliers goes out of business or the loss of key personnel creates organizational chaos that takes time and effort to resolve.

- **A clear need exists**   Other reasons for change are triggers such as legal or governance initiatives. For example, changes to the tax laws might require immediate attention, or government oversight initiatives such as the Sarbanes-Oxley Act[10] in the United States and Basel iii[11] in Europe might force an organization to alter its infrastructure and business processes to be in compliance.

- **Dissatisfaction with the status quo**   Dissatisfaction with the status quo is the primary reason for change. This might occur within an organization when its overhead is high and its competitive position is weak. In response, the organization might change business processes to have workers charge projects directly to reduce overhead. Such changes, in turn, might cause morale problems as workers scurry to find a charge number.

- **Embracing a new corporate vision**   When new executive leadership is hired, new vision often follows. Such leadership changes often result in other changes as the organization is altered to embrace the new vision. For example, the organization might make subsidiary organizations responsible for Profit & Loss (P&L). As another example, everyone in the organization might be trained in Six Sigma[12] concepts as a quality-focused culture is built.

- **Tackling a new mission**   Change might also be needed to cope with new mission statements. For example, the organization's management infrastructure might have to be altered if the organization decides to outsource maintenance because it can acquire needed support overseas at a fraction of the in-house cost, even when additional oversight and direction are required.

- **Moving to new business models**   Changes are often necessary when new business models are introduced, such as the software-as-a-service model. Organizational and infrastructure changes might be needed to increase the focus on the customer base when organizations move to a fee-for-service model to fund internal groups.

- **Building one culture**   When firms grow through acquisitions or mergers, building a single culture can become a problem. Changes that embrace "best of class" practices might be needed to facilitate getting the new divisions or personnel working together. Initiatives embracing common technical, managerial, and support processes, methods, and tools might be pursued to make single-culture goals a reality. Organizational structures and infrastructure might also be changed to accommodate partitioning the work to multiple groups. Selling off parts of the organization can also impact culture as organizations make adjustments to accommodate transitioned components.

- **Making a paradigm shift**   Software groups always seem ready to embrace a new paradigm, such as Agile methods or the Team Software Process.[7] Such methods represent a paradigm shift away from traditional approaches, which often are viewed as having too much structure and rigor. To accommodate the shift, lots of other changes are often needed in practice, which requires organization, process, product, and personnel changes in order to institutionalize the paradigm shift.

- **Expanding operations**   As they grow, software groups take over new space and facilities in geographically dispersed locations. New geographic locations often are added during acquisitions and mergers. As this happens, communications and coordination challenges confront them. Needs also materialize for new organizational and management infrastructures as they try to form teams and break down communications barriers. This is especially true when these organizations embrace new methods and paradigms such as Agile.

- **Eliminating waste and inefficiencies, and improving quality** A target area for improvement that often forces change is reduction of waste and inefficiencies, and improving quality. Based on my experience, software workers are not bashful about suggesting improvements. They take their jobs seriously and want to get their tasks done in the most efficient and "coolest" manner, as well as eliminate errors. Their recommendations for improvement can range from simplifying a task to automating tasks to adopting new technology to get the job done cheaper, faster, and better. They also will suggest getting rid of nonproductive work when it is boring and a waste of time.

As this list highlights, the primary reasons for change are business related. Yes, change must make good technical sense. But change needs to be aimed at improvement in order to get stamps of approval. That is why I dedicated an entire step in the change process in Figure 1-2 to justification. Independent of its impact, you must show that the proposed change makes a difference. Otherwise, it will not be either approved or pursued.

Why is it so difficult to change organizations?

There are many barriers—real and perceived—to change in software organizations. The ten barriers I have seen that occur the most often are listed here:

- **Comfort with the status quo** Probably the biggest barrier to change is comfort. People just do not like change. Or they believe that their organization, or at least the part they are part of, is successful enough. Change requires them to expend effort and do things that are unfamiliar. They would rather do routine tasks because the comfort level is high. Techniques exist that can be used to build momentum for change and motivate workers to do things differently. These require planning so that they can be budgeted and managed properly.

- **Change is mandated from the top** Another challenge is when management dictates change. Sometimes, it does not matter that the change is not needed. Management believes the change is necessary and therefore requires staff to do something they neither embrace nor believe in. For example, management might believe expenses are too high, and in response, they offshore the software work to cheaper operations. However, management might have been able to cut expenses more easily if they had asked the staff to suggest money-saving ideas. This works especially when local jobs are on the line.

- **Executive lip service** In this case, changes are approved without clear support from executive and mid-level management. In these circumstances, it is difficult to identify the requisite champions to make the change successful. Although management might pay lip service to the change, they do not actively support the project and do not budget accordingly. The result is instant failure. Without sponsors, changes tend to die because of interference, budget problems, and personnel problems.

- **Appropriate resources are not available** Another sign of problems is when you see the money, people, and facilities needed to implement the change assigned elsewhere. This often means the change initiative does not command the priority it needs to succeed. It also means that access to those needed to make the change and to opinion leaders will be limited. In my experience, this is a sure sign the change initiative is in troubled waters.

- **Organizational structures that do not facilitate teamwork and cooperation**   Change is about teamwork and cooperation. Building momentum and a groundswell for change tends to be more important than individual efforts. This is especially true in organizations that are happy with the status quo. "Why change?" those in opposition will ask. "The reasons are obvious," will be the answer posed by the team. "Because it represents a better technical and more practical approach," will be their mantra.

- **Inappropriate reward systems**   Another barrier to change is the reward systems. "What is in it for me?" is a common question posed by the opposition. "I can do the job much quicker and better using the existing practices," is their all too common justification. Some form of reward—ranging from the excitement of learning the latest and greatest technology on a pilot project to either cash awards or nonmonetary rewards such as plaques, t-shirts, or being recognized in the company newsletter—go a long way in most organizations.

- **Power politics**   Sometimes, change initiatives get caught in power politics. One group is trying to somehow trump another one in the organization, and by taking control of the initiative this group gains a foothold into the other group's area. Perhaps another group is trying to get a bigger share of the budget, and they pursue the change effort even though they have no vested interest in the initiative. Instead, they want the increased budget so that they can apply it toward shortfalls in other areas. Both of these examples are really not about the change initiative. They are about gaining power in an organization through people and money. In these situations, the initiative will have to reinvent itself to gain the attention and support of the new masters.

- **Conflicting priorities**   Dangers to effective change exists locally as well as at the executive levels. One problematic scenario is when the initiative is assigned to a pilot project that is under pressure to meet an aggressive schedule with limited resources (money, people, facilities, key personnel, and so forth). Even if the initiative has additional people and money assigned to it, delivery schedules always win when push comes to shove because they are perceived as more important in most firms. The trick is never to select a pilot project that is under the gun in regard to delivery and resources. However, sometimes you do not have a choice. You have to do the best you can with what you get and try to be successful.

- **Too much, too soon**   Many organizations view a pilot project involving change as a means to embrace an entirely new way of doing business. Instead of focusing on one or two things, they try to get it all right at once by embracing ten or more new techniques or practices. For example, they might adopt a new language and methods as they move to a new paradigm such as Agile processes. In my experience, these projects often fail because they are too broad and too unfocused.

- **Too little, too late**   Other organizations embrace change as a savior. They might be trying to adopt the change because they are in an organizational death spiral. Unfortunately, the reasons for the spiral are often business related and have nothing to do with the change. An infusion of capital might be a better solution than the adoption of new processes. The addition of new products might be more meaningful than the adoption of new product standards or underlying technologies.

As the cases within this book highlight, many techniques have been devised to help organizations address and overcome these barriers. Luckily, many of these barriers are neither new nor particular to a software organization. Approaches that have been tried and have worked for others can be applied. The trick to making them work is to adapt these proven techniques so that they are applicable to the work software groups do, their mindsets, the practices involved, and the environment in which they operate (including the organizational structures and management practices used to manage them). What most organizations fail to realize is that they might have to alter their culture, policies, business practices, management environments, and sometimes even the staff assigned to the project to facilitate making such changes occur in practice.

Questions to be answered

This book takes the approach of teaching you about change through example. I will set the stage for each case discussed using the operating environment pyramid presented earlier in this chapter. (See Figure 1-1). My aim is to show how factors such as organization, process, people, and product standards influence success in realistic operational settings within both industrial and government settings. As part of each case, issues will be raised and actions will be taken to answer three to five important questions. Some of the questions I address include the following:

- What is a change agent, and why do I need one? (Chapter 1)

- When embracing change, who is involved and why is it difficult to implement? (Chapter 1)

- How do I facilitate organizational change in a large Information Technology shop that is resistant to transformation? (Chapter 2)

- How do I identify the influence makers within my shop? (Chapter 2)

- What approaches should I use when trying to justify a software process improvement program for a large bank? (Chapter 3)

- Do I really need a dedicated process group to implement my process improvement program? (Chapter 3)

- What are the issues involved, and how do I address them when moving to commercial off-the-shelf and open-source software in an industrial setting? (Chapter 4)

- How do I change the management infrastructure for a small defense project whose review and reporting requirements seem excessive? (Chapter 5)

- Is earned value reporting worth the effort on small projects? (Chapter 5)

- What approaches should I follow when changing the underlying computational infrastructure used in my business to service my clients? (Chapter 6)

- How do I measure the impact of the change when working within a service industry? (Chapter 6)

- How do I show that the advantages of cloud computing are worth the costs? (Chapter 6)

- How do I scale Agile methods to work on a large project that is geographically dispersed? (Chapter 7)

- What approaches do I use to deal with zealots of a particular methodology who do not want to adapt methods to the situation at hand? (Chapter 7)

- What practices do I embrace on a large defense project that is behind schedule because of staffing problems? (Chapter 8)

- How do I avoid having my government customer bring a team in to help me get back on schedule and budget? (Chapter 8)

- How do I convince the government that the replacement technology I am proposing is not too risky? (Chapter 9)

- Can I use the concept of *technology readiness levels* to my advantage when trying to get others to adopt new technologies? (Chapter 9)

- What three things can I do within a government maintenance environment that is funded at a fixed level to reduce turmoil because of budget limitations? (Chapter 10)

- Should I contract a software maintenance job or staff it organically within a government shop? (Chapter 10)

- How do I leverage a government grant to get academia to develop meaningful education and training in topical areas pertinent to my organization? (Chapter11)

- How do I address political barriers in an academic institution that I am using to develop training for a new technology? (Chapter 11)

- What are the generic lessons learned from the ten case studies? (Chapter 12)

- What are the ten secrets of success when dealing with change within both industrial and government settings? (Chapter 12)

- How do I get workers at different levels of the organization (seniors, managers, workers, and so forth) to champion change? (Chapter 12)

Summary

This chapter introduced you to the content of the book, its goals, and how it is organized. It also answered the questions "Why change?", "What are the barriers?", and "What process should you use?". The chapter also introduced you to the framework I will use to handle each of the case studies that follow and what key questions I hope to answer. References and web pointers are also provided because my goal is to illustrate through example how to address issues you might encounter when putting these change management fundamentals into practice operationally in your organization.

References

References cited within this chapter include the following:

[1] Phil Rosenzweig, *The Halo Effect* (Free Press, 2007). See *http://the-halo-effect.com*.

[2] International Organization for Standardization (ISO)/International Electrotechnical Commission (IEC) 12207, *Software Life Cycle Processes* (Information Technology, 1995).

[3] International Organization for Standardization (ISO)/International Electrotechnical Commission (IEC) 15504, *Systems and Software Engineering, Life Cycle Processes*, 2008.

[4] Mary Beth Chrissis, Mike Konrad, and Sandra Shrum, *CMMI for Development: Guidelines for Process Integration and Product Improvement*, 3rd ed. (Addison-Wesley, 2011). Or on the web see CMMI for Development, Version 1.3, *http://www.sei.cmu.edu/library/abstracts/reports/10tr033.cfm*.

[5] Mike Cohn, *Succeeding with Agile: Software Development Using Scrum* (Addison-Wesley, 2009).

[6] Philippe Kruchten, *Rational Unified Process (RUP): An Introduction*, 2nd ed. (Addison-Wesley, 2000).

[7] Watts S. Humphrey, *Team Software Process: Leading a Development Team* (Addison-Wesley, 2006).

[8] Robert B. Grady, *Successful Software Process Improvement* (Prentice Hall, 1997).

[9] Norman L. Kerth, *Project Retrospectives* (Dorset House, 2001).

[10] The Sarbanes–Oxley Act of 2002, Public Law 107-204, 116 Stat. 745, enacted July 30, 2002.

[11] The Basel iii Accord. See *http://basel-iii-accord.com* for more information.

[12] Thomas Pyzdek and Paul Keller, *Six Sigma Handbook*, 3rd ed. (McGraw-Hill, 2009).

Web resources

Applicable web resources that amplify points made in this chapter can be found here:

- Amazon has lots of offerings that provide more details on the fundamentals. Go to *www.amazon.com* and under Books search for *change management*.

- The Association of Change Management Professionals (ACMP) has just started conducting an annual global conference on the topic. Information on the inaugural event can be found at *http://www.acmp.info/conference*.

- As an example of training in organizational change management, the Change Management Institute offers courses and provides a primer on the topic. Go to *http://www.change-management.com* and check out their offerings.

- As an example of the many e-learning resources available, Webucator has courses on change management available at *http://www.webucator.com/management-training/course/change-management-training.cfm*.

- Several universities offer organizational change courses as part of their certification programs. As an example, New York University (NYU) has a course on this topic that can be found at *http://www.scps.nyu.edu/course-detail/LROD1-CE9348/20113/organizational-change-management*.

- Australia even has a college focused on change management that offers courses on the topic. See *http://www.changemanagement.edu.au/index.html*.

- The guide named "Change Management 101: A Primer" can be downloaded from *http://www.changemanagementresources.com/2010/11/24/change-management-101-a-primer*. It highlights actions that can be taken to address common issues that arise.

- Cisco has made a six-minute video on change management, which is available on the Internet at *http://www.youtube.com/watch?v=bG5na7JD7rE*.

- Lots of excellent reports, papers, presentations, books, and other resources are available on facilitating software process improvement from the Software Engineering Institute's website, which is located at *http://www.sei.cmu.edu/library*. These resources by design revolve around use of the Institute's framework for process improvement called the Capability Maturity Model Integration (CMMI).

- An interesting paper that provides principles fundamental to making organizational changes has been published by the Jet Propulsion Laboratory (JPL) of National Aeronautics & Space Administration at *http://trs-new.jpl.nasa.gov/dspace/bitstream/2014/10570/1/02-2625.pdf*.

- Another useful site containing some interesting discussion of change management and its fundamentals appears at *http://www.businessballs.com/changemanagement.htm*.

- An article entitled "10 Principles of Change Management" is available at *http://www.strategy-business.com/article/rr00006?gko=643d0*.

CHAPTER 2

Industrial Case: Organizational Change in a Large Information Technology Shop

Setting the stage

Our first case study occurs in an Information Technology (IT) department that is part of a large multinational firm that is performing poorly. To quantify performance, senior management engaged a well-respected consulting firm to complete a benchmarking study to assess the competitiveness of the IT department based on an internal study of the team's recommendations for reducing waste and inefficiencies. The consulting firm's study has identified the following five findings that show the performance of the shop is below the norms when compared to similar IT shops from the same industry:

- Productivity, as shown in Figure 2-1, as measured in function points per staff month (fp/sm), is 20 percent below the industry norm for projects over 10,000 function points.

- Quality, also shown in Figure 2-1, as measured in defects/function point (defects/fp), is 50 percent higher than the industry norm for projects over 10,000 function points.

- Cost, as measured by $1,000 ($K) per employee, is 40 percent higher than the industry norm. See Figure 2-1.

- Personnel turnover, as measured by percentage turnover annually (%/year), is 25 percent above the industry norm. Again, see Figure 2-1.

- When queried, users of the systems view IT department personnel as arrogant, unresponsive, and rude.

These findings are very disturbing to senior management. They planned to have the IT shop launch an Enterprise Resource Planning (ERP) software initiative to tie packaged business applications used throughout the firm together by using a common framework. Based on industry reports,[1,2] using these integrated applications has the potential to save the firm hundreds of thousands of dollars a year. Because of the importance of the ERP introduction, senior management wants to get the IT department, including those production and support organizations it has set up overseas to keep costs down, performing well before beginning any initiatives that could cause the ERP effort to fail.

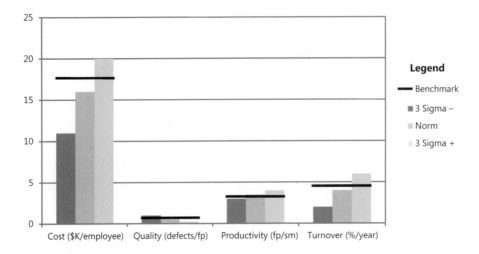

FIGURE 2-1 Performance of similar firms in like industries.[3]

In response, senior management has formed a problem-solving team to investigate the performance problems. This team is charged with finding the root causes of the performance problems and providing recommendations for improvement within 30 days. The team is led by the consultant who performed the benchmarking study because he, not the IT department, has credibility with the company's leadership. Other members assigned to the team are primarily support staff from the project management group— because the development units who produce server and user software say they are too busy working to get the next release out and they have no personnel they can spare for the study. For this case, assume you are a member of this project management problem-solving team.

Organization

This is a large, global IT organization. As shown in Figure 2-2, its operational units are dispersed across two continents with user front-end systems being developed in the United States, server software handled in Singapore, and customer support located in India. Releases from the two development sites are delivered to the United States and integrated in a common facility under the direction of a release management team. Each release is considered a project and, as such, is led by a project manager using staff from other units. While a server release may be generated in Singapore, it will be supported by product management, release management, and customer service personnel located elsewhere. There are approximately 1,800 professionals (architects, software engineers, managers, and so forth) and 500 support personnel (configuration management, quality assurance, and other such functions) working worldwide to provide IT support for the firm and its user base.

The systems provided by IT support a multinational firm with operating arms and sales offices in over 100 nations. These systems automate and integrate all of the firm's major business functions, which range from Customer Relationship Management (CRM) to Finance and Accounting (F&A) to

Human Resources Management (HRM). Although not state-of-the-art, the systems in use are up to date and functional and they perform adequately according to their users. Customers who use the systems are also primarily satisfied, but they constantly suggest upgrades because they view the systems as dated and neither state-of-the-art nor state-of-the-practice.

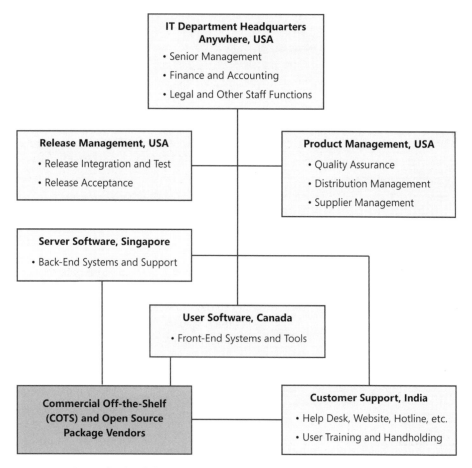

FIGURE 2-2 IT organizational chart.

Senior management's primary goal in moving to ERP in the future is to cut IT expenses through the use of commercial packages that provide similar functionality and performance at a fraction of the total life-cycle cost. However, management is not moving to ERP blindly; they have been briefed about many issues and risks. Because they recognize that the move to ERP will take time, investment, and considerable effort, they have planned and budgeted for the initiative accordingly. Even now, the planning team is working to determine how best to overcome the resistance within the company to moving to the new ERP systems that they are experiencing when they visit users in operating departments. Users of business systems throughout the firm do not want to change to ERP packages. They want management to leave things alone.

Project

The project's goal is to improve performance by identifying and recommending ways to put the IT organization's performance (using the measures used in the benchmark) on par with the competition, as illustrated by industry norms. The budget authorizes hiring three full-time people for a month. In addition to you, the team consists of the outside consultant and two company employees. All are seasoned veterans who are knowledgeable about the organization and its goals, culture, strengths, and shortcomings. Your team is lucky: one of the staffers is a person from the finance group who has access to the performance numbers for the individual organizational units, and the other is a quality-assurance person who has worked with the customers and understands what it takes to satisfy them.

During the kickoff meeting with senior management, management announces that they have some other goals for the project. They are extremely worried about the ERP transition. As part of your fact-finding efforts, they want you to identify what you perceive to be the barriers to change and to suggest ways to overcome them as the initiative gets started. In addition, they want you to take a hard look at the customer service organization in India because of complaints they have received about this department and to suggest areas of improvement. Even though you already have a full plate, you agree to tackle these new tasks because you really do not have any alternative.

Process

The process your problem-solving team will use to conduct its fact-finding chores is straightforward. Because of the time limitations and geographically dispersed offices it must visit, the team will conduct telephone interviews with key technical and managerial personnel. If possible, one or two of these interviews will be face to face. The team will gather facts during the interviews, along with opinions about what needs to be changed. Team members will ask questions about the transition to ERP, but they'll do so in a supplemental way. The consultant recommends that a checklist be prepared to structure the interviews and ensure that key areas of concern are not missed. Everyone agrees, and the consultant takes on the task of preparing the checklist, as others try to schedule talks with individual performers.

Product

The deliverable product in the exercise will be a briefing to senior management. The briefing is scheduled to last 30 minutes and consists of five or fewer slides. The consultant says that getting more than 30 minutes scheduled with senior managers is hard. However, if they are interested, getting them to stay longer is possible and the meeting could last up to an hour. The consultant also says that fewer slides are better when making a presentation to executives because this allows you to ad lib during the presentation and say things you do not want to put on paper.

The senior manager who asked you to investigate ERP asks the team to spend 15 minutes in her office. She wants to hear your plan of action. She also wants to relate to you the questions she wants answered during the briefing so that you can prepare answers for them beforehand. A second senior manager asks you to spend 15 minutes in his office. He warns you not to be too critical of the Indian operations. He initiated the offshore operations in India and is accountable for their performance, so you understand his concern. After this meeting, the consultant again takes the lead with the team and says it will be his job to deliver the unfiltered truth during the briefing, regardless of whom it might hurt. "After all," he says to the team, "that is why I was hired and put in charge of the study."

People

The initial interviews with various company personnel went better than expected at headquarters. People were frank and open, and they had lots of suggestions for improvement. Financial data that your teammate from the finance group gathered revealed a great deal about the performance problems:

- Most of the cost problems resulted from accounting practices used to compute overhead and depreciate capital equipment and software licenses.

- When productivity was computed, the formula used total staff size to determine staff hours. Function point sizing for the product was computed for changed code and new code. Reused and carryover code (unchanged code in the release that was integrated with the other code and retested) was not entered into the calculation.

- Twenty percent of the workforce was responsible for 80 percent of the productivity in the shops developing server and user software for the release.

- Eighty percent of the defects were coming from 20 percent of the systems, and these were clustered as expected in the user systems.

- Most of the turnover was occurring as staff members approached their five-year anniversaries.

Next, you held interviews with all of the organizations involved in the development of the ERP system, which are located in Canada, India, Singapore, and the United States. This took some doing as everyone seemed too busy to talk with you. You had to get the senior manager who chartered the study to intercede. Once scheduled, many interviews were postponed several times. When they did occur, people seemed guarded and their comments did not throw as much light on the problem as you would have liked. The sole exception was the operation in Bengalaru, India. The ten people you interviewed by phone were really candid about what the problems were and why they believed they were perceived as performing poorly in the area of customer support. Here is a summary of what you heard by location:

- **Canada: User Software**   The four leads you interviewed talked but said nothing. Instead, they pointed you to data that showed they were satisfying and even exceeding their cost, quality, and schedule goals. They were very defensive whenever anything negative was discussed. In addition, they did not perceive that they were performing below industry norms. They highlighted the fact that user systems are web-oriented and the rules for computing productivity and defect rates were different. They said that function points are not applicable because they use HTML and languages such as Perl and many of their systems have audio and video files on them along with smart help.

- **India: Customer Support**   As previously mentioned, the Indian interviews were very revealing because the people on the teleconference were not afraid to open up and share their problems with you. They stated that the root cause of their problems was a lack of training for their customer service representatives. Because budgets were so limited, the service representatives were given a single day of orientation when they joined the firm and then expected to begin working with customers. The division's English skills were good, as evidenced by test scores. However, American, Canadian, and Singapore English dialects and the context of situations they would be dealing with were not addressed in that single day of orientation. Their technical skills in web development were superb because many of their employees were graduates of premier Indian universities and held certifications in specializations like website design. Their knowledge of the Internet and available online resources was also excellent.

- **Singapore: Server Software**   The six people you talked with about server software disclosed that they had hard data to prove they were performing better than the norms. After the teleconference ended, they sent you spreadsheets with numbers that substantiated their claims. Because they were working on more traditional systems, most of the data submitted could be compared directly to benchmarks in the consultant's database. This situation seems very logical because the server software had been in service several years and the changes that were being made to it were primarily aimed at supporting updates being made to operating system and database management utilities. The one issue your team noted was that the software cost, quality, and productivity measures shared with you were computed differently. This group used industry standards like those published by the International Function Point Users Group (IFPUG)[4] to compute their numbers.

- **United States: Product Management**   When you talked with the product management people, they seemed to have nothing good to say about either the server or user software development shops. They stated that these software units used neither the processes nor the metrics that were developed and approved two years ago. These processes and metrics were created with representatives of each operating unit to satisfactorily comply with an International Organization for Standardization (ISO) 9000[5] audit that senior management forced the IT department to comply with. As part of this effort, process directives were published along with a process guide. Training was scheduled but delayed because scheduled releases got in the way. As a result, only a few people understood the process well enough to use it. The only seemingly positive output of the effort was the development of a common configuration and distribution management system and toolset that are in widespread use today in all of the software units across the organization.

- **United States: Release Management**   The five release management people you talked with had a different impression of the units developing server and user software. They complimented them on their team spirit as they related how interfaces between systems were specified and managed and how integration into common builds and releases was accomplished by the release team. They viewed the interaction across units in the IT department as very cooperative. However, their view of the web developers in Canada was not too positive. The software delivered by them was very defect-prone and difficult to understand. The release management unit had to expend a lot of effort to get rid of these defects as part of their integration testing. They also were not too thrilled with the customer support people in India. They found that there were a lot of user defect reports that could have been answered via the help line if not for their inadequate service. They believed that these problems could be rectified at the source. They were upset because the current release policy required that all problem reports had to be resolved before a release could be completed.

Options, recommendations, and reactions

The team decided to summarize the fact-finding results for the executive briefing using the three charts illustrated in Figure 2-3. The first chart was used to highlight the problems found in a way that was not threatening to the operational units. It suggests that software quality, not cost and productivity, are really the major issues. Software costs can be reduced by using a more pertinent set of accounting practices. For example, COTS software package licenses could be written off in the year acquired rather than being depreciated over a five-year period.

Software productivity is a numbers game where definitions can dictate results. In the case of the software benchmarking study, different software units in the company used different conventions to develop the numbers that were reported. For example, three different sets of conventions were used to count function points. Use of these different conventions resulted in deceptive results in the original study. When one set of conventions is used uniformly to develop the productivity numbers, as shown in the second chart of the briefing, they do not look so bad.

With regard to quality, the lack of a consistent process and the use of poor peer review and unit test practices led to relatively high defect rates. The poor customer service offered by personnel in India had an impact on quality. The poor quality code delivered by the user software unit in Canada to the release management unit in the United States also had a negative impact on software quality. Quality is, therefore, the area that the team identified as requiring immediate attention, and it should be the number one target for improvement.

The third chart highlights the major options and actions recommended by the fact-finding team. This chart allows you to talk about actions without getting stuck on the details. It also points management in the direction you want to lead them.

Two other charts are also provided for the briefing. Chart 4, presented next as Table 2-1, provides backup for this pitch to senior management. It summarizes the "top 9" issues in priority order and the actions recommended to be taken in case management asks for them during the briefing. The three items marked with a + represent the low-hanging fruit: these suggested changes can yield large results with little effort. Chart 5, shown in Figure 2-4, summarizes the team's recommended plan of action over the next two years for addressing the issues. (Getting funded for two years instead of one gives you more time to be successful.) The plan breaks down resistance to change by engaging key influence makers within each of the software units in the change process as members of the software working group. To minimize both software costs and potential impacts, the tactic of embracing actions as part of the move to ERP was advocated.

Key Findings

- Talked with all software groups

- Cost and productivity are not issues

- Quality improvement needs to be addressed

- Customer service personnel need training

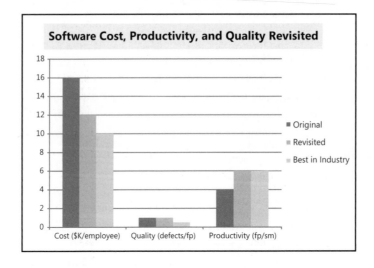

Software Cost, Productivity, and Quality Revisited

Major Options and Actions

- Do nothing

- Mount a quality initiative
  — Reduce defects
  — Improve customer service
  — Implement actions as part of plan to
     get ready for ERP

FIGURE 2-3 Executive briefing slides.

TABLE 2-1 "Top 9" Issues and Recommended Actions.

No.	Issue	Recommended Action
1	Poor quality: below industry norms.	Initiate a quality initiative. Collect defect data. Embrace Six Sigma concepts, and use the data to facilitate improvements. Create a budget for the initiative. Staff the core team, and use influence-makers to stimulate adoption.
2	Poor customer service: support personnel are viewed as arrogant and unresponsive.	Require customer service personnel to complete training before deploying them. Allocate dedicated training budgets. Monitor service performance.
3	Embrace a common gated process (that is, personnel must pass a review before moving from one task to the next) across software units.	Update the firm's ISO 9000 process to be more relevant, and stimulate its use throughout the company by making it a factor in personnel appraisals. Increase product management's budget accordingly to accomplish this.
4	Acquire and use more modern development methods and tools.	Encourage units to try Agile methods, and update toolsets used by teams to be more modern. Use tools to identify defect-prone and complex code, and eliminate it, especially in web-based user systems.
5	Adopt a common set of measures and metrics.	Define a common set of measures and metrics for both workers and executives. Make them part of the ISO process, and use existing tools to gather the data.
6	Use appropriate accounting practices+.	Work with finance to change how software costs are accounted for in operating budgets and Profit & Loss (P&L) computations.
7	Stimulate better teamwork and coordination.	Set in place a software working group, and have it devise common processes and identify common issues across the firm. Engage influence-makers as part of the working group. Provide feedback on what works and what does not.
8	Reward high performers+.	Work with the human resources department to put a series of both financial and nonfinancial recognition rewards in place for high performers. Aim these rewards at improving retention.
9	Embrace new personnel practices to reduce turnover+.	Meet and counsel personnel at five-year marks. Aim counseling at improving personnel satisfaction. Reduce turnover by helping employees to take on work they find interesting, helping them with career advancement, and working with them to increase job satisfaction.

Tasks	Quarters 1 & 2	Quarters 3 & 4	Quarters 5 & 6	Quarters 7 & 8
Form team	⟶			
Devise detailed plan	⟶			
Put gated process in place	⟶	⟶		
Define and report measures/metrics	⟶	⟶	⟶	⟶
Update business processes (for ERP)	⟶	⟶	⟶	⟶
Train customer service representatives	⟶	⟶		
Adopt new methods and tools to improve quality	⟶	⟶	⟶	⟶

FIGURE 2-4 Recommended action plan.

Outcomes and lessons learned

The briefing to management went very well. They liked what they heard and agreed with the recommendations made by the team. The action items listed in Table 2-2 were suggested during the presentation, and the plan to improve quality was tentatively approved based on the availability of funding. The questions posed during the pitch were anticipated because you conducted a practice meeting with the sponsor. These questions ranged from "Where will the budget for these actions be found?" (with the answer being, "It is a zero sum game, and your budget will not change") to "How do you identify the influence-makers?" (with the answer being, "That's easy: ask workers who they respect"). What surprised you was a heated discussion about the move to ERP at the end of the presentation. Senior managers were concerned that they were not ready for the move. Luckily, you were prepared by senior management's request to provide suggestions on how to tackle this seemingly hot topic. Basically, you advised management to revise their business practices as they slowly transition to ERP. The scary thing that you found in your research into the topic was that firms who tried to move to ERP all at once failed. Those who succeeded made the transition gradually. They got one system up and running before trying to implement the next one. Not surprisingly, the critical system identified was finance and accounting because it provides the information that many of the other systems require to work properly.

TABLE 2-2 Action Items Suggested During the Senior Management Presentation.

No.	Status	Action Item	Resolution
1	Open	Find funding for these initiatives.	Changes to accounting practices should free up some funds.
2	Open	Update the plan with details.	Will do once team meets.
3	Open	Meet with the accounting department, and help them change their practices.	Done: awaiting their closure.
4	Open	Meet with personnel, and identify needed changes to practices (reward high performers/aim at retention).	Done: awaiting their closure.
5	Closed	Form and start up an initiative team.	Charter and membership defined in advance of meeting. First meeting scheduled next week.
6	Open	Work on customer service issues.	Will do once funding is found to address training. Will form focus group to make other suggestions.
7	Closed	Identify influence-makers.	Asked performers, and they were more than willing to identify influence-makers. A memo has been sent.
8	Closed	Identify high performers.	Asked managers, and they specified the people they valued most. A memo has been sent.

The lessons learned in this industrial case were many. They include, but are not limited to, the following:

- When identifying issues affecting cost, productivity, and quality, dig deep to identify both the issues and their root causes.

- Use industry benchmarks from reputable sources to establish baselines for comparison.

- When working in highly political environments, use consultants to serve as independent, unbiased, and reputable sources.

- Be suspect of definitions because by making slight changes to them you can make your performance look good (or bad).

- Look for the obvious and the low-hanging fruit when pinpointing issues that affect performance. You will be surprised how simple fixes have big consequences.

- Remember that quality is king. Customers will not return if your company has bad service and defective products, even within captive organizations like Information Technology shops.

- Improvements will always take longer than expected. The reasons for this are simple: motivating change is hard, and breaking down barriers takes time.

- Influence-makers represent an important mechanism for change in most organizations. Identifying them is easy: all you have to do is ask the performers.

- When making changes, recognize that some aspects of a change are easy and others are difficult. Do the easy things first because success with them gives you a boost and builds momentum for the harder changes. Also, early successes can be advertised and used to motivate people for future action.

- Senior managers are unpredictable. Getting their attention and support takes a lot of strategy. Because their plates are full, you have to set the priority on what you are trying to do. Establishing such priorities means that you have to relate your goals to that of the business.

Summary

This chapter provides you with some insights into preparing recommendations for a senior management presentation. As you probably expected, there are lots of politics and subagendas you should be aware of. Some of the suggestions you raise when dealing with senior management are subtle. For example, make sure you have a sponsor to serve as a buffer for you at such meetings and to provide you advice on how to package the materials. Other suggestions are obvious. Go into the meeting prepared with detailed backup information. The suggestions offered in this case are real and represent normal findings when you get involved in change and improvement. Make sure you pick the low-hanging fruit. This tactic allows you to gain credibility by achieving quick successes. Also, as in the case presented in this chapter, understand that most improvement and change initiatives are viewed as threats by peer organizations within the company. Because your budget comes from funds that could have gone into someone else's pocket, you will make enemies of those who were denied funds, regardless of the merit of your proposals.

References

References cited within this chapter include the following:

[1] Bret Wagner and Ellen Monk, *Enterprise Resource Planning,* 3rd ed. (Course Technology, 2008).

[2] Thomas F. Wallace and Michael H. Kremzar, *ERP: Making It Happen: The Implementers' Guide to Success with Enterprise Resource Planning,* 3rd ed. (John Wiley & Sons, 2001).

[3] Capers Jones, *Software Assessments, Benchmarks and Best Practices* (Addison-Wesley, 2000).

[4] International Function Point Users Group (IFPUG), nonprofit, member-governed group aimed at promoting and encouraging the use of function points; see *http://www.ifpug.org.*

[5] ISO 9001, *Quality Management Systems—Requirements* (International Organization for Standardization, 2008).

You might also be interested in these references:

More Secrets of Consulting (Dorset House, 2001), by Gerald Weinberg, provides readers with good advice for changing organizations.

My book *Making the Software Business Case: Improvement by the Numbers* (Addison-Wesley, 2001) provides insight into how to develop the numbers when preparing to address senior management in situations like those represented in this case.

Web resources

Applicable web resources that amplify points made in this chapter can be found here:

- Amazon has a lot of books on subjects discussed in this chapter. Search for *software benchmarks*, *software measurement*, *software process improvement*, and/or *software quality*.

- Gartner Research has some interesting resources for those trying to measure IT efficiency and effectiveness and conducting site surveys, such as the case here: *http://www.gartner.com/4_decision_tools/measurement/measure_it_articles/dec01/mit_ite_v_ite.jsp.*

- The Chief Information Officer website has lots of resources for those interested in Enterprise Resource Planning at *http://www.cio.com/article/40323/ERP_Definition_and_Solutions.*

- My 2004 benchmarking paper is one of the most referenced sources for such data in the industry; see *http://www.compaid.com/caiinternet/ezine/Reifer-Benchmarks.pdf.*

CHAPTER 3

Industrial Case: Justifying a Process Improvement Program for a Large Bank

Setting the stage

The second case I'll present involves a large bank that has over 10,000 offices, with a presence on every continent (including Antarctica, where the bank has an automated teller machine). Its Information Technology (IT) department provides its clients with a full range of services, from bill paying to commercial loans to payments in foreign currency.

The IT department has a new director, who joined the company about a month ago from a competitor. As his first act, he immediately replaced the heads of all the operating departments with people from his prior bank. He justified the personnel changes using the fact that the IT department had consistently missed its release deadlines during the past two years. Because nobody seems to know what will happen next, morale has dropped to an all-time low. It is a good thing that jobs in the banking industry are scarce. Otherwise, a lot of the good people would be leaving.

At the all-hands meeting at headquarters, the new director introduces his staff. Next, he spells out his new vision for the IT department. He is a firm believer in process. He believes the organization has been too lackadaisical about its software processes. To better service the bank's customers, he wants the organization to use a common software process. A reliable process is needed to address changes required as increased governance is applied by regulatory agencies worldwide. Such governance is constraining how banks and financial institutions operate. He is looking for a few volunteers to work as part of a team that will define, deploy, and institutionalize a well-defined and disciplined set of software processes within the next six months. Those who apply, he says, should have appropriate experience introducing processes in similar large organizations. He also describes how he hopes to use the process to streamline operations and cut the fat from the organization. Being lean and focused on customers is what management is after.

Organization

The current organizational structure is pictured in Figure 3-1. New organizations that the director is proposing appear in the shaded boxes in the figure. As in many other banks, project management within the IT department is centralized, with operations in three locations. Software development is done in New York City, where the corporate headquarters are located. The mega-computing center, where all processing is handled, is located in Raleigh, North Carolina (NC). This center is also where all application releases are built, tested, and deployed to various bank sites (ATMs, branches, and other outlets). To keep costs under control, the bank has located customer support and its associated call center in the Philippines. As shown on the organizational chart, because of its importance to him, the new director is creating a process organization that will report directly to him.

The two new proposed organizations include the process group and the project management group. The process group will be responsible for defining, rolling out, and institutionalizing software development processes and best practices for the organization at the institutional level. They will train personnel in the use of the processes as the group refines the processes based on user feedback. They will employ statistical process controls to optimize the use of processes and be responsible for the measurement and metrics reporting. They will work with the quality assurance (QA) group and independent test groups (ITGs) to automate the metrics data collection and reporting processes.

The project management group represents an attempt to implement a matrix management[1] concept, where one organization is responsible for product development and another group is responsible for the timely delivery of quality products on schedule and budget. This arrangement allows the development group in New York City to focus on helping its staff develop the right skills to perform the required technical tasks and the project management group to focus on delivery schedules and budgets. Under such an arrangement, skilled personnel who are needed for applications development on a part-time basis—for example, personnel working on escrow-related applications—can be shared across projects. The project management group will also serve as a liaison with customers and regulators to ensure that their requirements are satisfied as the applications are built. This is a critical function for the firm because the ramifications of failing to adhere to governance in a bank can result in massive fines and penalties.

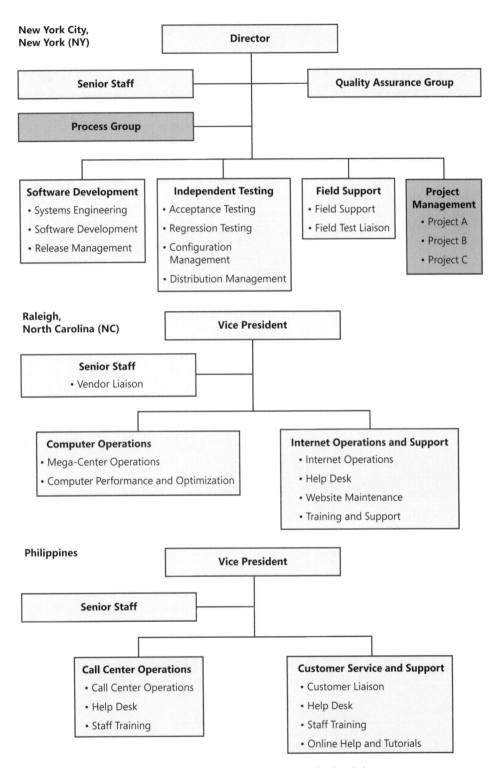

New York City, New York (NY)

Director

Senior Staff

Quality Assurance Group

Process Group

Software Development
- Systems Engineering
- Software Development
- Release Management

Independent Testing
- Acceptance Testing
- Regression Testing
- Configuration Management
- Distribution Management

Field Support
- Field Support
- Field Test Liaison

Project Management
- Project A
- Project B
- Project C

Raleigh, North Carolina (NC)

Vice President

Senior Staff
- Vendor Liaison

Computer Operations
- Mega-Center Operations
- Computer Performance and Optimization

Internet Operations and Support
- Internet Operations
- Help Desk
- Website Maintenance
- Training and Support

Philippines

Vice President

Senior Staff

Call Center Operations
- Call Center Operations
- Help Desk
- Staff Training

Customer Service and Support
- Customer Liaison
- Help Desk
- Staff Training
- Online Help and Tutorials

FIGURE 3-1 Bank Information Technology (IT) department organizational chart.

Project

You find out that you have been assigned to the process group because you are one of the few people in the firm with experience defining and deploying institutional processes. You view this as good news because you want to make a contribution. You attend a kickoff meeting that very afternoon and learn more about your new assignment. The process group is organized as shown in Figure 3-2, with you as the full-time person addressing metrics and measurement. As shown in the figure, seven people are assigned to the group, four full-time and three part-time. The lead was selected because she is a good manager, has process experience, and is trusted by the director. Two senior people who have been with the firm for over ten years have been assigned to write processes. A part-time curriculum designer has been assigned to develop training processes, and two retirees who have credibility with the troops have been hired as part-time consultants to facilitate the transition of the processes into practice as the project management organization gears up and takes control of developmental tasks. This situation beats the ones you experienced in the past, where process group members were chosen based on their availability and not their experience. This meant that the group was staffed by subpar performers.

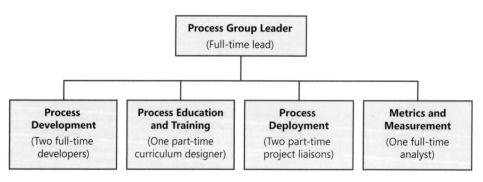

FIGURE 3-2 Process group organization and personnel resources.

As a relatively new person in the bank, you also learn that process improvement initiatives have been tried in the past with limited success. As shown in Figure 3-3, it has been a rocky road for process improvement within the bank. According to the old-timers, the reason for past failures is that required executive support did not last because of conflicting priorities and changing directors. With the new director pushing hard for software process improvements, everyone on the team believes that the chances for success are high this time. Based on the bank's history, your only hope is that the new director stays in place long enough for the team to succeed.

FIGURE 3-3 Process improvement history at the bank.

Process

As a first order of business, the team meets to develop its plan of action for the process improvement effort. Because the team has existing process resources to start with, everyone agrees that developing processes and training should not take more than a year. Because putting the new processes to work in a matrix organization is difficult (because many interactions are required across groups to implement them correctly), the team allocates two years for this effort—one year for early adopter projects, and the second year for the remainder of the projects. Because the groups in Raleigh, NC, and the Philippines neither develop nor maintain software, it is suggested at the meeting that they be excluded from the effort. But their participation is deemed important by the process group lead because they need to use many of the same support processes developed for the rest of the firm, such as configuration management, quality assurance, and supplier management (including vendor liaison) in order to achieve institutionalization. The suggestion to exclude them is therefore rejected.

The second major decision made at the meeting was to use Capability Maturity Model Integration (CMMI)[2] as the framework for assessing process maturity and improvement. There was lots of discussion over alternatives, especially ISO 9001.[3] When the discussion reached an impasse, the team lead decided to resolve the issue by asking the director whether he had any preferences regarding a framework. The director told the team to use CMMI because he had experience with it in his previous position and it worked fine.

Product

Your team briefed the director yesterday on its plan. He liked the plan, but told your team he is under pressure to defend the cost for process improvement from opponents who do not want to allocate funds for it. Based on their past experience with process improvement efforts at the bank, the opponents are arguing that the effort does not make sense economically and the money could be spent better elsewhere. The director needs ammunition to win this battle. He asks you to prepare a cost justification for his use.

The product of this exercise, therefore, is a justification for the process improvement effort in terms of the benefits that are forecast to be derived across the IT department. The process lead says that the two-year planning horizon you have planned for should be adequate. As the measurement and metrics lead, you are asked to perform the task within the next three days.

People

To develop the justification, you will have to determine a realistic cost-benefit analysis for the effort. Determining the costs is easy because all you have to do is look at the budgets that you developed in the plan to come up with a tally. A summary of these forecasted expenses, which are about $1.9 million a year in today's dollars, is provided in Table 3-1. Entries in the table assume that personnel costs are $180,000 of effort per year for each person assigned to the project (without general and administrative costs and profit added). As an example, process development costs in the table assume the lead and two developers will be charged to this account (three people at $180,000 per year each).

These figures assume the forecasted personnel expense increases will be kept in balance based on the cost of money (that is, today's dollar is worth less than tomorrow's due to inflation). Other assumptions are provided as footnotes to the table.

TABLE 3-1 Annual cost summary for the process improvement initiative.

Task	1st Year's Cost (in thousands)	2nd Year's Cost (in thousands)	Total Cost (in thousands)
Process definition (development and update)	$540	$540	$1,080
Project support[a]	$360	$360	$720
Training (development and conduct)[b]	$300	$180	$480
Metrics and measurement (development and analysis)	$180	$180	$360
Assessment support[c]	$250	$250	$500
Collaborator meetings and participation[d]	$180	$180	$360
Promotion and outreach[e]		$200	$200
Website development (including tools)[f]	$100	$10	$110
TOTALS	**$1,910**	**$1,900**	**$3,810**

[a] Two retirees providing project support because they have instant credibility
[b] Purchase rights to courseware plus project leads to train project personnel in the process
[c] Conduct Standard CMMI Appraisal Method for Process Improvement (SCAMPI)[4] assessment using outside contractor
[d] Provide charge number for collaborators to support the process improvement effort
[e] Handle the public relations necessary to get people to use the process (includes e-newsletter)
[f] Purchase specialized software to put up a website with open and secure areas

A web and literature search yields lots of hype on the benefits of process improvement.[5,6] Most process improvement models are so large they do not seem credible. However, several approaches used to compute benefits seem to be worth trying. The first of these computes the amount of additional work your IT development staff could complete with incremental increases in productivity of 10 and 20 percent. This approach seems reasonable because annual releases of some of your products to the field are scoped based on the number of changes and repairs, the work to be accomplished, and the work that can be made with a fixed workforce. You decide to pursue only this one approach because of time limitations. Again, results are due in three business days.

Because you want to tailor the justification to the audience, you ask your lead "Who will review the cost/benefit analysis?" Your lead says that the numbers will be reviewed in depth by the director's senior staff members. These staffers include financial, legal, and other non-technical advisors who work on contracts and budgets for the director. The reviewers will look mainly at what benefits will accrue. It is a tough audience because they do not always understand the difficultly of the technical tasks that are behind the returns. Based on these observations, you know that the numbers you present must be solid. Otherwise, there will be turmoil as you try to explain your position.

Accelerating productivity

You decide to use your current productivity of five function points per staff month of labor as your starting point to demonstrate the gain associated with process improvement. Productivity in this sense is defined as the ratio of outputs (as measured in function points) to inputs used to generate them (staff months of labor). Based on the work of Brad Clark at the University of Southern California,[7] you find that the average annual gain in moving from one CMM level to the next is about ten percent. In addition, the Software Engineering Institute (SEI) has published results[8] that show it takes between 19 and 24 months to move up a maturity level. Using these data sources, you can realistically assume that you can jump up one level if the bank's process improvement program is succeeding. Because you hope to make several jumps, you extend the timeline to five years. Your assumption that you will realize a ten percent gain in productivity during each jump seems reasonable, and you plan to accelerate productivity by using it to compute cost avoidance. Cost avoidance is preferred because it looks at eliminating future costs, not those that are more immediate. For example, cost avoidance would investigate eliminating hiring of new people in the future instead of laying off staff immediately to bring the costs down to reflect productivity gains. Based on these assumptions, you compute the benefits achieved by accelerating productivity through use of the CMMI (as portrayed in Table 3-2) to be an average of $4.08 million annually, assuming a five-year planning horizon and a cost of money of 3 percent. The director suggested that you discount the benefits attributed to the process improvement initiative to take the cost of money into account to keep the financial people on his staff happy.

TABLE 3-2 Savings attributed to accelerating productivity from 10 to 20 percent annually.

Savings Worksheet	Year 1	Year 2	Year 3	Year 4	Year 5
Current productivity (function points/ staff month), gaining 10% annually through nominal means	6.0	6.6	7.3	8.0	8.8
Accelerating productivity gain of 10% annually after a one-year startup period	No gain	7.2	8.6	10.4	12.4
Additional work, expressed in function points, that can be performed assuming the firm employs 1,000 software professionals	No gain	600	1,300	2,400	3,600
Cost avoidance ($3,000/function point)[a]	No gain	$1,800,000	$3,900,000	$7,200,000	$10,800,000
Cumulative cost avoidance	No gain	$1,800,000	$5,700,000	$12,900,000	$23,700,000
Present value of investment assuming a 3 percent cost of money	No gain	$1,700,000	$5,200,000	$11,500,000	$20,400,000

[a] Computed from $15,000/staff month divided by 5 function points/staff month

Looking at the costs and benefits, you see an annual return of $4 million for expenditures of about $1.9 million a year during the five-year planning horizon. The projected return on investment (ROI) during the first five years, assuming no adjustments for the cost of money, is calculated as follows:

ROI = Annual Returns ÷ Investments = $4M ÷ $1.9M = 210% in the second year

Note that you are representing savings as cost avoidance. The materials you have read[9] about developing business cases suggest this approach because cost avoidance focuses on future expenditures while cost savings represents immediate savings. This means that with cost savings you take immediate actions, rather than future actions, to cut costs. For example, you might lay off staff rather than avoid making a future purchase to achieve your savings goal.

Options, recommendations, and reactions

The new director asks you to make your presentation to him before sending it out for review. You heard through the grapevine that his push to improve processes is under attack from peers who represent the bank's IT system users. They would rather see the money put into customer service improvements such as self-help and training. The director likes what you present. However, he suggests that you bolster your case by identifying several feasible options, including defect reduction, and by looking at intangible benefits. Of course, you agree. Defect reduction is a brilliant idea because it directly addresses concerns others have about customer-directed upgrades.

After considerable thought, you determine there are three feasible alternatives that should be presented in your analysis. The first is to justify investments in process improvement by using early defect detection and correction. Next, you can show how process improvement initiatives benefit the organization as it continues its move to commercial off-the-shelf (COTS) software packages and using a contractor workforce rather than an employee workforce. The third alternative is to do nothing and invest the money in some other initiative, like one centered on improved customer service.

The first option proves relatively easy to build a case for because the IT department has been collecting defect data for the last five years. As part of earlier process initiatives, it defined measures and metrics and captured the data automatically as part of their configuration management (CM) process. Unfortunately, the IT department has not done anything with the data for the last two years, and you will have to mine it to get the facts you need for evaluating this option. After about two weeks, you find that the average number of defects being reported a month worldwide are about 800. These are distributed by location and priority, as shown in Figure 3-4 for a typical month. Based on the data collected, it takes about 40 staff-hours and costs about $4,000 per defect to find and fix a defect. If you can reduce high-priority defects (categories 1 and 2) by ten percent a year, you can avoid $80,000 in costs annually—(10%) (800 defects) ($4,000/defect) = $320,000 cost avoidance. Although this does not save the bank enough money to justify the costs of process improvement, it does show an added benefit.

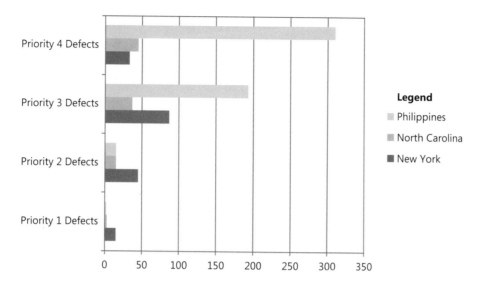

FIGURE 3-4 Typical defect distribution by location and priority.

Figure 3-4 assumes that defects are classified using the priority scheme summarized as follows:

- **Priority 1**   A catastrophic defect that must be fixed or the system will either crash or be discredited by auditors and for which there is no known workaround.

- **Priority 2**   A critical defect that must be fixed or the system will fail to work properly and for which there is no known workaround.

- **Priority 3**   A serious defect that must be fixed for the software to operate properly.

- **Priority 4**   Any of a number of annoyance defects that are found and fixed in a release. Annoyance defects typically are those that result in user/operator inconvenience.

The large number of Priority 4 defects being logged in the Philippines is a concern because these represent customer service issues.

The second option focuses on the cost side of the equation. You can justify your process initiative by reducing your direct software labor costs. You can make a strong argument that moving to commercial off-the-shelf (COTS) software packages and contract (either local or offshore) labor resources without strong processes would be a disaster. However, after much study you determine that any savings the bank will realize during the first six years of operations will be offset dollar for dollar by the additional costs incurred for startup, licensing, COTS selection and tailoring, oversight, and contract management. For example, even in the best of circumstances, you estimate it will take about a $3 million investment and a year to scope requirements, run a competition, and select COTS vendors and labor contract suppliers because of the oversight required by senior bank management and regulators. Then you will need at least another $3 million and two years to start up your contract labor organization and license, tailor, configure, and pilot the use of the COTS packages prior to employing them operationally at a cost of $1 million per year. This estimate includes the effort you will need to mount in parallel to set in place supplier and contract labor management personnel and practices. It also assumes that no benefits will accrue until the third year.

Based on these startup estimates, it does not seem that the push to use COTS packages and contract labor will save enough during the near term to justify the costs of process improvement. Initial benefits will not be derived until the third year if the bank is lucky and, as Figure 3-5 shows, the breakeven point for the investment does not occur until the start of the sixth year. However, it does help build a compelling business case should the bank decide to pursue such a cost savings initiative in the long term in conjunction with making process improvements.

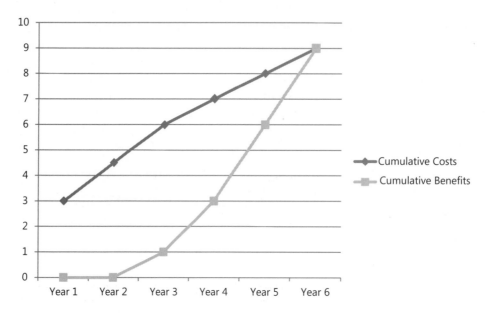

FIGURE 3-5 Breakeven analysis for COTS package and contract labor option.

The do-nothing initiative is a no-brainer. Neither savings nor cost avoidance will be achieved via this option. Yes, better customer service might result. However, such service improvements do not translate directly into either IT cost savings or cost avoidance. More direct action, such as mounting a software process improvement effort or a defect reduction initiative, is needed to achieve these goals. Therefore, the do-nothing initiative is not a feasible alternative for IT when belt-tightening is their primary goal. However, as a secondary goal, better processes could stimulate better service. This answer seems like a good retort to those opposing the director.

Outcomes and lessons learned

All of your preparation paid off. The meeting with the director's staff went exceptionally well. There was lots of discussion and, of course, several people took the floor to show the new director how smart they are. But, after almost three hours of discussion, everyone agreed it made good business sense to pursue the process improvement initiative. The financial expert said he could find about $1 million to start the effort later this year. The process group lead was ecstatic and shook your hand after the meeting saying, "Good job."

Of course, you also presented the action items listed in Table 3-3. The most controversial of these items at the meeting was whether or not the bank needed a dedicated process group to pursue the initiative. This issue was resolved in favor of having the process group, as most initiatives that used part-time resources failed in the past because of lack of focus. The actions remaining are primarily aimed at arming the director with the ammunition he will need when he battles for resources with his peers. Although he has the startup funds, he wants to ask for new funds to cover the initiative instead of taking it out of existing budgets. This means that senior bank management will have to take the funds from someone else's allocations next year and beyond. Everyone is cheering for the director. Even if they are not a fan of focusing on processes, they are in his corner and want to help him succeed. You will pursue the action items and provide the materials requested as soon as you possibly can.

TABLE 3-3 Action items taken during the director's staff review.

No.	Status	Action Item	Resolution
1	Open	Provide a table with intangible benefits to supplement tangible ones.	Will provide for the director meeting with his bosses.
2	Open	Provide fallback plans if only $1 million is made available to fund process improvement.	Will provide for the director meeting with his bosses.
3	Open	Provide a detailed cost-benefit and cash flow analysis for the early defect detection and COTS and contract labor options.	Will provide for the director meeting with his bosses.
4	Open	Have a present-worth analysis available for the early defect and COTS and contract labor options.	Will provide for the director meeting with his bosses.
5	Open	Review additional analyses with financial staff prior to sending it forward to the director.	Will provide for the director meeting with his bosses.
6	Closed	Justify the use of a dedicated process group for handling the initiative. Why won't part-time resources work?	Experience of others was brought forward to provide requested justification.
7	Closed	Identify other banks that pursued similar process improvement initiatives, and note their outcomes.	Compiled list was provided to the director at the meeting.
8	Closed	Identify resources that are available to conduct assessments and help with the training.	Compiled list was provided to the director at the meeting.

The lessons learned in this banking case were many and include, but are not limited to, the following:

- When pursuing process improvement, it is helpful to have a framework like the CMMI and ISO 9001 to organize it around.

- Understand that most barriers to implementing software process improvement are psychological and behavioral. Practical strategies that help you lead during turbulent times are needed[10] to address these barriers.

- To win the battles of the budget, it is important to come to the fight armed with a business justification for your expenditures, an idea where you will find the money, and a plan for achieving desired results.

- You also need to have credible historical data available from your industry on which to base your justification for expenditures.

- You also need to pre-sell your justification to the approval authority and others who influence the decision.

- Ask those who review and endorse your submittals for change for their help when you're preparing requests for money and approval. If they agree to help, they have no option but to support your requests through the authorization process.

- Having a champion at the corporate level is a plus in any industrial environment.

- When preparing justifications, make sure there are no errors in your calculations. A single mistake can destroy your credibility when dealing with audiences discussing budgets that are offset against their finances.

- Remember, allies today are enemies tomorrow especially when funding is on the line.

Summary

This chapter arms you with some tools for preparing business justifications for a process improvement initiative. As expected, such justifications are needed to get organizations like the bank in this case study to make major expenditures in process and infrastructure improvements. The case embraces cost avoidance as its primary tool because it aims justification at dodging costs in the future, not the present. It also illustrates use of return-on-investment techniques that can be used to emphasize the financial benefits associated with making such improvements. The case also highlights the politics involved as organizations try to get internal funding for changes. Getting money is always hard. It takes strategy, guts, and perseverance to succeed in the battle of the budget.

References

References cited within this chapter include the following:

[1] Jay R. Galbraith, *Designing Matrix Organizations That Actually Work: How IBM, Procter & Gamble, and Others Design for Success* (Jossey-Bass, 2008).

[2] Suzanne Garcia and Richard Turner, *CMMI Survival Guide* (Addison-Wesley, 2006).

[3] ISO 9001, *Quality Management Systems—Requirements* (International Organization for Standardization, 2008).

[4] Dennis M. Ahern, Jim Armstrong, Aaron Clouse, Jack R. Ferguson, Will Hayes, and Kenneth E. Nidiffer, *CMMI SCAMPI Distilled (Addison-Wesley, 2005).*

[5] Dennis R. Goldenson and Diane L. Gibson, *Demonstrating the Impact and Benefits of CMMI: An Update and Preliminary Results,* Software Engineering Institute, Report No. CMU/SEI-2003-SR-009, October 2003.

[6] Wes Covell, "The Benefits of CMMI," *Proceedings CMMI Technology Conference,* Denver, CO, November 17, 2009.

[7] Bradford Clark, *The Effects of Process Maturity on Software Development Effort,* University of Southern California, Center for Systems and Software Engineering, Report No. USC-CSE-97-510, Ph.D Dissertation, August 1997.

[8] Carnegie Mellon University, *Process Maturity Profile,* Software Engineering Institute March 2011. See on the web: *http://www.sei.cmu.edu/cmmi/casestudies/profiles/pdfs/upload/2011MarCMMI.pdf.*

[9] Donald J. Reifer, *Making the Software Business Case: Improvement by the Numbers* (Addison-Wesley, 2001).

[10] *Managing Change and Transition,* Harvard Business Press, Boston, MA, 2003.

Web resources

Applicable web resources that amplify points made in this chapter can be found here:

- Again, Amazon has a lot of books on subjects discussed in this chapter. Go to *www.amazon.com* and search under the terms *software business cases*, *software process improvement*, and *software quality*.

- Of course, the Software Engineering Institute (SEI) at *www.cmu.sei.edu/library* has lots of relevant reports and resources available in its library to help you to understand, justify, and use the CMMI in process improvement activities.

- The SEI also maintains the Software Process Improvement Network (SPIN) Directory at *http://www.sei.cmu.edu/spin/*, which lists process improvement professionals in a given geographic region who are engaged in such activities.

- As you would expect, the International Organization for Standardization (ISO) also provides resources to help understand, justify, and use its standards in practice at *www.iso.org*.

- The Data & Analysis Center for Software (DACS) has a multitude of resources available to support process improvement at *http://www.thedacs.com/databases/url/key/39*. These include lists of best practices, experts, service providers/consultants, and other items.

- An excellent report titled "Measurement for Process Improvement" by Joyce Statz and published by the Practical Software and Systems Measurement (PSM) group is available at *http://www.psmsc.com/Downloads/TechnologyPapers/PI_Measurement_v1.0.pdf*.

- Process improvement conferences are held in the United States and Europe annually under the auspices of the SEI that publish a lot of relevant information. For information on these conferences go to *http://www.sei.cmu.edu/sepg*.

CHAPTER 4

Industrial Case: Moving to Commercial Off-the-Shelf and Open-Source Software Usage in Telecommunications

Setting the stage

This next case study occurs in a large telecommunications firm. The firm wants to move from a custom architecture to an open architecture for its Switching Systems division's product offerings. This division has resisted past attempts to make a move to a new platform and architecture because it had millions of dollars invested in specialized software, which its sales and management leadership viewed as a discriminator in the marketplace. Because of new sales opportunities, the firm initiated the development of a new switch that embraces many innovative concepts. By bringing this switch to market, the firm hopes to retain its market share and position in the future. Everyone in the firm's organizational chain, depicted in Figure 4-1, agrees that it is time to make the changeover and do it right.

The key change being proposed is a move to a new architecture and an open system platform. As shown in Figure 4-2, the applications software will run on top of a POSIX platform riding on top of multiple processors, which execute in parallel to provide growth paths in case more lines need to be added by telephone operating companies (the customers). POSIX will be configured to run using existing facilities to provide platform-designated services on an on-demand basis. Such services include, but are not limited to, configuration and initialization, relational database management, dispatching, distribution, querying, scheduling, and security. Services will run to completion to avoid interrupts that could cause execution to stall, stop, or be rescheduled.

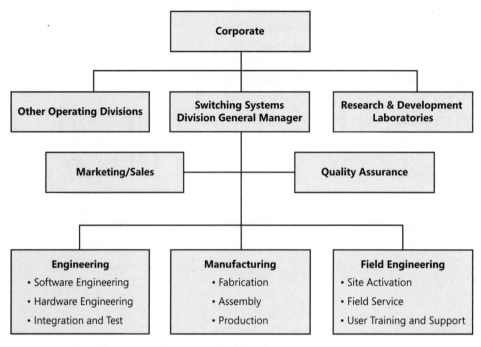

FIGURE 4-1 Telecommunications firm organizational structure.

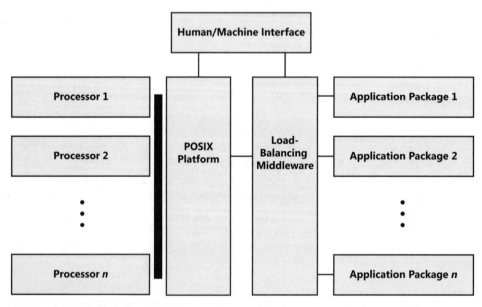

FIGURE 4-2 Top-level switching system architecture.

In addition to using normal switching applications, the new system will provide users with a novel, knowledge-based, self-regulating load-balancing dispatcher and an innovative self-diagnosis and repair system that will act as the marketplace discriminator for sales. The front end of the switch will provide a wide range of network-based and Internet-accessible communications capabilities. It will provide users with easy access to features and query-on-example ability. Context-sensitive help will be provided along with many improved user-interface features to make the system intuitive, easy to understand, and fun to use.

The two key innovative technical enablers that make it feasible to build such a system now are the following: new dispatching algorithms that the Research and Development (R&D) Laboratories invented that facilitate the optimum scheduling of application threads running on parallel processors, and new middleware that allows the system to bind components together using rule-based, load-balancing techniques. Components that are scheduled are fragments of applications packaged by the middleware to execute in parallel on different processors (parallel threads) and share results (self-combinations). Application fragments can include commercial off-the-shelf (COTS) components, open-source or custom routines, modules, or programs, as long as each scheduled and combined entity adheres to the packaging rules, runs under POSIX, and uses the system's data model.

Organization

For this case study, assume that you are the lead software engineer in the Engineering division responsible for developing the new switching system. The initial target of opportunity for sales of the system is a telephone operating company that is your largest customer. This company worked with your people on the architectural specification for the system and helped generate the related functional and performance requirements for it. It wants to buy 100 of these switches, assuming that your organization can deliver them within three years. It is ready to help during the development in any manner possible. The company suggests that it perform the independent verification task, where it provides feedback during the development on the products as they incrementally roll off the drawing board.

Most of the work that the Switching Systems division currently performs is aimed at supporting systems in the field. Major developments like the new system come around once a decade. As such, this represents the means to update the organization's processes, practices, methods, tools, skills, and experience. Management, however, recognizes that by doing too much too quickly your company could fail. In response, they want to attack the development conservatively and use only proven technology. They form a task team to devise a project plan, and you are asked to be a member. You are thrilled and ready to start contributing to the effort.

Project

The project being planned involves the design, development, and validation of a test article that will be used as the model for product development. The development is targeted for three years. Getting manufacturing facilities ready for production will take about year. However, this can be accomplished easily in parallel with the product development because the production facilities are ready for use.

There are no budget details yet. Because the future of the division revolves around the success of this project, you believe management will allocate whatever resources are necessary to pull it off. Even though their funds seem limitless, management wants you to justify every penny.

The planning team is made up of the following six people: you, the team lead, a financial person, the chief engineer, a process person, and a customer representative. Besides several other responsibilities, you have been asked to handle all planning activities associated with COTS and open-source software. Everyone on the team is excited and wants to do a good job.

Your team assessed the current situation and found that both systems requirements and architecture specifications for the new system have been completed by the startup team. These specifications were reviewed as a first order of business and judged to be well done. The team also found that a feasibility study was completed that identified 26 candidate COTS and open-source application software packages for potential use on the project.[1] Several of these candidates have been analyzed on a try-before-you-buy basis, and the results were documented. During development, you know you will still have to select packages, negotiate licenses, and integrate these packages as part of the switching system. You also know that your work with COTS and open-source software will not stop here. There will be annual updates and licensing costs to worry about after the system is operational. Licensing concerns you because there might be run-time license costs associated with some of the packages that have not been accounted for.

Based on this completed work, the team feels much better because their planning efforts would not have to start at square one. In addition, the startup team has completed a high-level budget of $770 million over the three-year development schedule and determined details of the first year's operation in the field, which appear in Table 4-1. As part of your tasking, you are asked to review COTS and open-source forecasts to determine whether or not they are realistic for the job at hand.

TABLE 4-1 Top-level budget for new telecommunications system development and maintenance.

Task	Subtask	Forecasted Budget by Year (in millions)			
		Year 1	Year 2	Year 3	Year 4
Systems engineering	System engineering plan and trade studies	$10	$10	$—	$—
	Integration product team operations	5	10	5	—
Project management	Project management	20	20	20	—
	Measurement and analysis	2	2	2	—
Product support	Configuration management	4	4	4	—
	Quality assurance	4	4	4	—
	Supplier management and licensing	2	2	2	—
	Security and network protection	3	3	3	—
Hardware engineering	Hardware acquisition and readiness	10	10	10	—
	Interface development and test (both hardware and software)	10	10	10	—

Task	Subtask	Forecasted Budget by Year (in millions)			
		Year 1	Year 2	Year 3	Year 4
Software engineering	Requirements analysis	$10	$5	$—	$—
	Software development	25	50	50	—
	COTS and open-source package acquisition and readiness	5	10	10	—
	Software integration and test	10	10	10	—
	Licenses	2	2	2	—
System integration and test	Test planning and readiness	10	—	—	—
	Hardware and software integration and testing	—	25	25	—
	System test and evaluation	—	—	10	—
Manufacturing	Specification	8	3	3	—
	Test article fabrication, assembly, and production	20	25	25	—
	Production article fabrication, assembly, and production	—	25	25	—
Systems test	Test article testing	—	10	10	—
	Acceptance test and evaluation	—	—	10	—
Deployment	Staging and delivery	—	—	25	—
	Dual operations and cutover	—	—	25	—
Operations and maintenance	Planned product improvements (both hardware and software updates and optimizations)	—	—	—	75
	Licenses	—	—	—	5
TOTALS		**$160**	**$240**	**$290**	**$80**

Process

Your next step in the planning process is to determine what work needs to be accomplished to get the product out, determine who will do it, when it will be done, and at what cost. The team lead suggests that the team use a divide-and-conquer strategy to develop the work plan, where each member of the team develops a task list for different parts of the effort. Of course, you are given the COTS and open-source package work as part of your assignment. Your job is to determine whether the line item totals under "Software engineering" titled "COTS and open-source package acquisition and readiness" and "Licenses" are adequate to cover the work required to be completed in these areas.

You first identify the tasks required to employ COTS and open-source packages[2] in the development. Completion of these tasks assumes that the middleware performs as specified and that each package can be cleanly integrated into the system without any rework other than tailoring. The process model used to describe the activities being performed to put COTS and open-source software to work throughout the life cycle is shown in Figure 4-3.

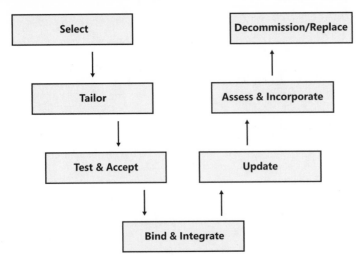

FIGURE 4-3 COTS and open-source package software process model.

For those unfamiliar with terms used in the process model in Figure 4-3, a brief explanation may be in order. After you select a package, you typically configure and tailor it to satisfy your requirements using built-in features. Then you test and accept the package prior to taking delivery. Once you've accepted it, you bind the COTS package via your middleware to your system, integrate it, and make it work with the system at large. Next the vendor provides periodic updates that you evaluate and incorporate into your system, if appropriate. You continue in this mode until you decide it is time to either replace the package with an alternative or decommission it.

The wildcard in the case is the unique data model your people have devised. You must determine whether or not the package can be tailored to accommodate it prior to making your purchase decision. Luckily, this was one of the tasks the startup team performed during the trial licensing period. They assessed the candidate packages to make sure that they worked as advertised and were compatible with the architecture's data-model specifications. You feel relieved when you discover these facts in the notes they provided to you.

Product

You complete your analysis based on the process model shown in Figure 4-3. Based on the selection of the 12 packages listed in Table 4-2, you clearly show that there is more work that needs to be performed than the budget allocated for the packages being considered. The major reason for the cost differential seems to be the run-time licenses for packages for system software (such as the database manager) and tools (such as compilers and debuggers) that operating companies want delivered in case they have to make patches in the field. In addition, as shown in the itemized list in Table 4-2, the budget for COTS and open-source software package licenses is low during software maintenance because many of the development tools and other support licenses were not included in the estimate. The people developing these forecasts overlooked these costs because the costs were not in their frame of reference (software development vs. maintenance).

TABLE 4-2 Itemized costs for COTS and open-source packages.

No.	Package Type	Development License Cost	Maintenance Cost (plus run-time licenses)
1	System software (POSIX toolset)	$250,000	$800,000
2	Database management toolset	$250,000	$2,200,000
3	Requirements management and traceability toolset	$100,000	$100,000
4	Software design toolset	$50,000	$50,000
5	Software language toolset (compiler, and so forth)	$500,000	$1,500,000
6	Software test toolset (coverage, and so forth)	$250,000	$250,000
7	Hardware CAD tools	$500,000	$500,000
8	Software configuration management tools	$250,000	$350,000
9	Test management toolset	$250,000	$250,000
10	Computer performance evaluation toolset	$250,000	$250,000
11	License management toolset	$50,000	$50,000
12	Documentation toolset	$200,000	$200,000
	TOTAL	**$2,900,000**	**$6,500,000**

People

You deliver your findings, and they get incorporated into the project plan. After conducting a peer review, the team lead asks you to prepare some backup materials on COTS and open-source packages because most of the team believes that upper management is clueless when it comes to the issues associated with their use. In response, you develop Table 4-3 to summarize the reasons your firm should buy rather than develop custom software packages, and Table 4-4 to highlight the typical risks associated with the purchase option and related strategies that have been used to successfully mitigate them.[3] These backup charts are received well by the team as the effort to get the plan out concludes.

TABLE 4-3 Developing software in-house vs. licensing it.

Develop Software In-House	License Software
You pay the total development and maintenance cost.	You pay only a fraction of the development and maintenance costs.
Custom software takes years to develop.	Software is available immediately.
The product is mature and relatively bug-free.	It takes considerable time to mature the product.
It's developed to satisfy your customer's requirements.	It's primarily developed to satisfy marketplace requirements.
It's easy to change because you are in charge of the migration path.	It's harder to change because market forces drive the migration path.

Develop Software In-House	License Software
It's hard to determine whether or not the software, when built, will serve the customer's needs.	It's easy to assess what capabilities exist and prototype with existing packages.
Your team must provide user support, training, and documentation for the software.	The package comes with support, training, and user documentation.

TABLE 4-4 Top 10 risks and related mitigation actions taken with licensing software.

No.	Risk	Mitigation Action
1	Hidden license costs.	Understand licenses, and negotiate favorable terms prior to signing the licensing agreement.
2	Package capabilities are not as advertised.	Assess package capabilities via a trial license prior to licensing.
3	Architectural feature mismatches might be present (different data models).	Make sure that you fully assess the package candidates before signing a license agreement.
4	The software architecture puts a premium on performance rather than adaptability.	Modularize the architecture around foreseeable sources of change and the use of COTS.
5	No control over the migration path.	Establish a relationship with the vendor to influence the migration path.
6	Poor customer service.	Pay for on-site support or premium service contract.
7	Most times, all that you get is the executable, not the source code.	If it's really critical, negotiate for a source-code license.
8	The vendor might go out of business.	Establish a market watch to identify replacements, and get the source code put in escrow in case of vendor default.
9	Software upgrades are not in synch with your update cycles.	Architect products using COTS and open-source packages to accommodate such updates.
10	Better alternatives appear on the market, but you are locked into this vendor.	Maintain flexibility in licensing, and keep a market watch.

Options, recommendations, and reactions

You believe that you have everything you need to ask for more money to cover the tasks associated with the use of COTS and open-source software on the development project. You have a rationale for using packaged software, a risk mitigation plan, a package selection list, plus a rationale for your choices, a task list for the work involved, and an associated cost estimate.

You are absolutely shocked when comments are received on the plan. Reviewers from the engineering department sliced your package selection rationale apart. They provided a more technical analysis that justified the use of custom rather than COTS and open-source packages for everything except the system software. They argue in detail that the risks associated with using someone else's software are unacceptable because of performance and security issues. They further suggest that COTS and open-source software cannot be segmented easily to run on parallel processors even with their new scheduling and dispatching software. They point to vendor websites and blogs to provide evidence of security vulnerabilities and breaches that occurred in most of the packages. Based on the input, there is no doubt in anyone's mind that they want to develop the software in-house. When you talk with the team to find out why, you get a big surprise. Several teammates tell you the reason is that the engineering department has a declining workload. They believe the department is using the new development project to justify the jobs for hundreds of people who will be laid off if packaged software is used for the new system.

You are caught in a quandary. You believe that going with COTS and open-source software is the right decision, but you do not want to be responsible for layoffs. The team lead understands your dilemma and suggests that the decision be elevated to senior management. According to the grapevine, engineering department leadership is already working the issue and is using their influence to squash the use of COTS and open-source software in the new system.

You decide the best way to compare the custom options against the COTS options is to look at the time and effort required to complete them. Then, if management wants to ignore the facts, that is their decision. You develop Table 4-5 to make the results easy to comprehend. For simplicity, you include only the software-related development costs across the three-year project schedule. To develop a credible development estimate, you use the parametric COCOMO II cost model[4] using the standard estimating practices endorsed by the firm. Size estimates are those that engineering developed while performing a study to determine how many processors would be needed to accommodate peak loading on the new switching system. Results have been scaled proportionately for support tasks like product and project management using similar percentages.

TABLE 4-5 Custom vs. COTS and open-source software development comparison.

Task	Custom Software Development		COTS and Open-Source Package Usage	
	Schedule (months)[a]	Effort (in millions)[b]	Schedule (months)[c]	Effort (in millions)[d]
Systems engineering	6	$ 25[e]	6	$ 30
Project management	Level of effort	75	Level of effort	45
Product support	Level of effort	55	Level of effort	30
Software engineering	66	370	24	201
System integration and test	12	55	12	30
Systems test	3	10	3	10
Deployment	3	5	3	5
TOTALS	**72**	**$595**	**36**	**$351**

[a] Tasks will be done in parallel to achieve delivery in 3 years.

[b] The shortest feasible schedule according to COCOMO II model as calibrated is 6 years.

[c] Effort was computed using a nominal profile for telecommunications and a size base of 4 MSLOC (million source lines of code). Cost/staff-year of effort is assumed $200,000.

[d] Numbers were taken from Table 4-1 in this chapter and scaled to include software costs only.

[e] COCOMO II model estimates the cost is less than the estimates submitted by the engineering staff.

Outcomes and lessons learned

The numbers in Table 4-5 tell the story. Developing custom software doubles the schedule and adds $244 million, or about a 70 percent increase in costs, to the effort. Yes, there might be risk in using COTS and open-source software. But there is lots of risk in pursuing a custom development as well.[5] Also, the desired three-year schedule for the project is infeasible if you use custom development.

When you review your numbers with the planning project team, they are impressed. But your team lead is not. He says the battle has just started and that you better check and double-check your numbers. He suggests that the engineering department will use every trick in the book to discredit you. Power, jobs, and budget are on the line. Therefore, the fighting will be fierce. He asks the member of your team from the finance group to dig up past engineering costs to determine if the cost model's assumptions are in line with actual results. He then asks the team if they know of any metrics that senior management uses to test estimates. The response is that the magic number used in the firm for validation is $100 per SLOC (source line of code). Where that figure comes from nobody knows. However, when you apply it, the results of using this rule of thumb seem to compare nicely with the $92.50 per SLOC that was the output of the cost model ($370 million divided by 400 MSLOC).

The financial person on the team reports his findings, which are surprising. The cost per SLOC actually delivered six years ago for the switching system that is currently in the field was $125 per SLOC. When you think about it, you can build a case that you would expect current costs to be less, especially because you plan to exploit advances that have been made in technology when you build the new system. You and your boss feel comfortable about your numbers and feel ready to defend them when management calls you as they try to settle the debate over the use of COTS and open source. In the interim, you plan to research the numbers more completely in an attempt to further validate your findings. Your strategy is to let the numbers do the talking.[6] Management can ignore them if they want, but they paint a compelling case for the use of COTS and open-source software packages in the new switching system. As a change agent, you also need to recognize the need to use techniques to address resistance.

The lessons learned in this telecommunications case were many and include, but are not limited to, the following:

- COTS and open-source software represent new ways of doing business. As such, you should apply change management principles to enable early, frequent, and ongoing communications with stakeholders to deal with the inevitable resistance that will be encountered.

- There are many advantages and disadvantages associated with the use of COTS and open-source packages. Be sure to evaluate each carefully before making a commitment.

- COTS and open-source software packages do not come for free. Besides the license costs, there are other expenses associated with getting the package ready to be interfaced and used as part of the system in which it will operate.

- When looking to use COTS and open-source packages in systems, be sure to identify and license all of the packages you need in the systems, applications, and support domains during development, maintenance, and operations (run-time licenses).

- Recognize that most COTS and open-source packages do not plug and play directly out of the box. Some effort might be needed to configure, tailor, integrate, maintain, and sustain these packages throughout the life cycle. This is especially true if there are architectural mismatches and the packages do not support your data model.

- Maintenance of COTS and open-source software packages can be difficult because they are updated at a different frequency than the system they are part of. In response, you have to plan to synchronize package updates with your releases and map the features.

- Plan also to try to influence the direction COTS and open-source software package vendors take through relationship management. Although you might not be the vendor's biggest customer, you want to be one of their most important ones. Realize that you might have to pay a premium or make investments to achieve this status.

- When performing a make/buy analysis as in the case study, recognize that the numbers will do the talking unless there are compelling reasons why they should be discarded.

- Take care to make your numbers believable and credible. Whenever possible, validate them against your past performance and rules of thumb that are part of your firm's history.

Summary

This chapter provides those who are planning projects with insights into how to spot, quantify, and deal with controversial issues. Controversy in planning almost always revolves around risk. "Risk" in this sense is defined in terms of exposure to adverse effects, schedule delays, or cost excesses. Because risk can make change more difficult, it should be considered carefully. Once risk is quantified, the trick in risk management is to let the numbers do the talking. I have seldom seen management select the most costly option. In those rare situations where I have, there has been some urgent business reason like keeping an operation afloat until a new contract is negotiated or a takeover attempt has been consummated. In this case study, the really risky and difficult issues associated with COTS selection, tailoring, integration, and sustainability were not even brought to the table. The reason for this was simple. If I had raised these issues, this chapter would have taken too much space and still might not have provided a proper treatment. However, be careful with evaluating COTS solutions, and realize that they need to be handled carefully. When and if you do use COTS and open-source solutions, you'll see why I provided you with a warning.

References

References cited within this chapter include the following:

[1] Kurt C. Wallnau, Scott A. Hissam, and Robert C. Seacord, *Building Systems from Commercial Components* (Addison-Wesley, 2002).

[2] Scott Hissam, Charles B. Weinstock, Daniel Plakosh, and Jai Asundi, *Perspectives on Open Source Software*, Software Engineering Institute, Report No. CMU/SEI-2001-TR-019, November 2001.

[3] Paul Clements and Linda Northrop, *Software Product Lines* (Addison-Wesley, 2002).

[4] Barry W. Boehm, Chris Abts, Winsor Brown, Sunita Chulani, Bradford K. Clark, Ellis Horowitz, Ray Madachy, Donald Reifer, and Bert Steece, *Software Cost Estimation with COCOMO II* (Prentice Hall, 2000).

[5] C. Ravindranath Pandian, *Applied Software Risk Management: A Guide for Software Project Managers* (Auerbach Publications, 2006).

[6] Donald J. Reifer, *Making the Software Business Case: Improvement by the Numbers* (Addison-Wesley, 2001).

Web resources

Applicable web resources that amplify points made in this chapter can be found here:

- Amazon has many books and articles on subjects discussed in this chapter. Go to *www.amazon.com* and search under the headings of *COTS*, *open source*, *product lines*, and *risk management* to find relevant citations.

- The Software Engineering Institute (SEI) at *www.sei.cmu.edu/library/* also has many citations on these subject areas because they happen to be an interest area of their primary customers.

- A briefing by Dorothy McKinney about the pluses and minuses of COTS use is available at *http://www.incose.org/northstar/2001Slides/McKinney%20Charts.pdf*.

- An interesting case study about COTS software has been prepared by the faculty at McGill University and is available at the following website: *http://www.cais-acsi.ca/proceedings/2000/beheshti_2000.pdf*.

- A COTS Risk Mitigation Guide developed by the Federal Aviation Administration in 2010 is available at *http://fast.faa.gov/docs/COTS%20Risk%203.1a%20Guide.doc*.

- A briefing article about COTS security vulnerabilities by Craig Miller of Cigital is available at *https://buildsecurityin.us-cert.gov/bsi/623-BSI.html?branch=1&language=1*.

- Another briefing about COTS hardware and software for NASA's Earth Observing System can be viewed at *http://edhs1.gsfc.nasa.gov/waisdata/rel6/cd71560001_4.pdf*.

- Information about the Open Source Initiative (OSI), which is a nonprofit corporation whose mission is to educate and advocate for the use of open-source software, is available at *http://www.opensource.org.*

- A comprehensive manual describing how to develop open-source software for Intel's PCI Express family of gigabit Ethernet controllers can be viewed at *http://download.intel.com/design/network/manuals/316080.pdf.*

CHAPTER 5

Industrial Case: Small Defense Project Needs Help

Setting the stage

Asmall commercial software firm specializing in applications software security won a Small Business Innovation Research (SBIR) program Phase I contract from a defense agency about ten months ago to validate algorithms that detected and protected software binaries against reverse engineering attacks. The SBIR program[1] fosters commercialization of products that government agencies need through a three-phase program. Phase I validates feasibility. Phase II is aimed at proof of concept, while Phase III pursues commercialization with private sector support.

Reverse engineering attacks attempt to disassemble the binaries to develop a replica of the software design so that those interested in it can understand the software logic and data structures, build better competing software products, and/or find and exploit vulnerabilities in the future.[2] The customer viewed the firm's recently completed $100,000, six-month, SBIR Phase I contract as successful. Because of this, the firm's Phase II proposal for a $1 million, two-year effort to build a prototype toolset that enables the firm to prove its concept by automating its process for inserting the protection into the executable has been accepted. The firm hopes to use the prototype to convince others of the potential of the concept. It is currently negotiating a contract for the new Phase II effort with the agency's buyer. The award process was put on the fast-track because the firm was able to attract matching funds of $500,000 from a larger software house specializing in software security. All that this firm wanted for its investment was rights of first refusal for the commercialization of the technology. With the government contract award, the total funding for the effort will therefore be $1.5 million.

This is a big win for this small firm. Its largest contract in the past was its Phase I award of $100,000. This award was negotiated as a fixed-price labor hourly contract, where the firm billed time and material expenses directly to the government and were paid monthly based on its customer representative's approval of the firm's invoices. Although the firm had to go through a few hoops to get the contract, the result was very rewarding. The firm got to perform exciting research with a minimum of overhead and bureaucracy.

Organization

The firm is a small business with ten employees. It has a relatively flat organization with seven professional employees who do just about everything. Officers of the firm are techies who prize their security expertise, networking knowledge, and practical problem-solving skills. Besides performing research and development (R&D) efforts, the firm offers a range of products and services in the software security field. For example, the firm performs vulnerability analyses for customers on a time and materials basis to identify security weaknesses in client policies, practices, systems, and procedures. As part of these analyses, the firm also performs penetration testing to pinpoint problems in systems that need to be fixed immediately. As another example of its offerings, the firm conducts a variety of training for its clients, ranging from one-day and two-day seminars to mentoring with an on-the-job-training component.

The remaining three employees include an office manager, a part-time bookkeeper, and a part-time intern. The office manager keeps the office operating at peak efficiency and makes sure computers and other equipment are up to date and working. He also answers the phones, orders supplies, and does proofreading. Besides keeping the firm's books, the bookkeeper prepares the invoices and handles payroll every two weeks. She also maintains expertise in the firm's accounting software. The intern is a full-time student majoring in computer science at a local college who does whatever odd jobs pop up. These tasks include running errands, making copies, installing software, and updating the firm's website.

Project

As already mentioned, the Phase II SBIR contract is the largest award that the firm has ever received. It represents a significant piece of work because it will extend for two years and fund three to four people full-time. Because of the potential awarding of the contract, the firm is already trying to hire two more professional employees. Candidates have been identified, and they are being courted in hopes that they will join the firm when the contract is finally awarded. Hiring new employees represents a significant effort on the part of the officers and is causing a significant decline in current billings, which is having an effect on cash flow. In a small firm like this, every hour spent on overhead tasks like interviewing and performing reference checks results in an hour not billed.

The office staff is getting things ready for a government audit next week based on materials provided by the auditors.[3] In anticipation of awarding your firm the contract, the government identified the following materials that it wants to review:

- History of past performance on government contracts

- General policies and procedures

- Finance and accounting practices

- Security procedures and training

- Project management practices and reporting

- Subcontract management practices, including those for people working as consultants

During the visit, the auditors also want to look at the articles of incorporation, past corporate tax returns, current operating expenses, accounting ledgers, and payroll records. They are especially interested in officer pay and remuneration, including bonuses, use of the company car, and stock options. Needless to say, there is a lot of paper involved and the staff is busy getting it ready for review. They have spent the last couple of days copying materials and preparing packages that the government auditors can review and take home with them.

Process

For this case, assume that you are an officer of the firm that wrote the winning proposal and will lead the project once the contract is finally awarded. You learn that writing the winning proposal is just the first step in the government contracting process. When you research the topic[4] more fully, you find that the next step is the issuance of a draft contract and then negotiations. Once the contract's terms and conditions are agreed to, a contract can be issued.

You also discover that government auditors are visiting you to determine if you have the ability to perform and complete the deliverables that you promised in your proposal. They are reviewing your records to determine whether the labor rates, overhead expenses, general and accounting (G&A) rates, and profit that you offered in your proposal are reasonable and appropriate for a research contract of this size and nature.

Needless to say, it is panic time. In addition to all of the paperwork the staff has assembled for the auditors, you and your colleagues have to work all weekend to get your records in order. You believe that you have built a convincing story to justify why your forecasted labor, overhead, and G&A rates for the contract are higher than those you have had in the past. You read that fairness is the underlying principle for negotiations. You believe that you are ready for the visit.

The government auditors show up, and they are all business. They dig deep and want copies of just about everything imaginable. In response, the firm's intern has spent the entire day making more and more copies for them. They ask a lot of questions, especially as they have you defend the rate structure in your proposal. Other areas of particular interest to them are officers' compensation, including the use of the company car, whether you have foreign nationals working for the firm, what equipment and software you will buy using contract funds, and the details of your 401K retirement plan. They spend time confirming that the overhead and G&A rates were 97 percent and 6 percent during your last fiscal year. They also confirm that government business represented 17 percent of your revenue on average during the past two years.

Product

About two weeks after the visit by the auditors, you receive an e-mail with the name and phone number of the government buyer and a draft contract. When you read it, you are amazed. The contract is 142 pages long and contains lots of boilerplate text taken from a model contract that is used as the standard for larger cost-plus-fixed-fee contract awards. You read it twice and try to understand what it says, to no avail. Finally, in desperation you call the firm's attorney and ask him whether he has dealt with large government contracts before. Because the Phase I contract was simple and fixed-price, no legal review was performed in the past. He says he has not, but refers you to another lawyer who has expertise in such agreements. You contact this attorney, and he agrees to review the contract. However, he wants a retainer of $4,000 up front before he will begin. Of course, you pay because you have no other option. The government agency wants your response within 15 days.

Two weeks later he comes back with his analysis. He says the contract is typical of those used for $1 billion acquisitions. It has the following provisions that you need to be careful of:

- It is a cost-plus-fixed-fee contract with a fee of 6 percent.

- The total dollar value of the contract is what you proposed. However, the number of labor hours authorized is 20 percent more. When you ask him to explain what this means, the lawyer says that the government did not accept your proposed rates. Instead, they adjusted the rates to reflect your past-performance actual results, which were 20 percent less than the bid rate you proposed.

- The contract has a monthly progress payment of 80 percent of the actual cost. When you ask the lawyer to explain what this means, he says it means that 20 percent of the actual cost and all of the profit will be held in reserve until the contract is completed and the actual costs are determined via audit. He informs you that this is a standard clause in cost-type contracts.

- The contract has a key personnel clause that states the government has the right to approve replacements for key personnel. When you ask who these people are, the lawyer says it is everyone who was named in the proposal as major contributors. That is everyone in the firm.

- The contract has a "no foreign labor" clause, which means that all people who work on the effort must be US citizens. Two of your people are foreign nationals who are permanent residents working on green cards.[5] Your intern, who is here on a student visa, is also a foreign national.

- The contract has many intellectual property provisions. Because it is an SBIR contract, you will receive commercial rights to any technology you develop or patent. However, the government will retain limited rights to the technology and will be entitled to take delivery of it via a no-cost license once it is commercialized.

- The contract requires lots of reporting. The lawyer says reports are a standard means to establish interim deliverables to which progress payments are linked. However, the number seems excessive. In addition to monthly progress and funds status reports, you are required to deliver an average of two to three other technical reports a month as well.

- The contract requires earned value reporting[6] using a validated system within 60 days of the contract award. Associated reports will be delivered monthly thereafter.

- The contract requires that your finance and accounting systems be validated prior to use by the government.

- The contract requires that 10 percent of the funds be spent with minority contractors.

- The contract requires that you comply with equal opportunity laws and be certified as such.

- The contract requires that you will not use convict labor in the performance of the effort, will not use ball bearings manufactured outside the United States, and other such items of importance. These terms are inserted in order for the agency to be in compliance with the law.

- The contract requires that the customer approve all publications about the contract prior to their release to the public. This includes press releases, articles, technical papers and reports, and even website notations.

- The contract requires that you get a facility security clearance in case some of the potential collaborators in Phase II are working on classified contracts. Once such a clearance is acquired, you will be required to get those working on the contract cleared as well.

The lawyer's report is 20 pages long. It lists over 100 restrictive clauses like those listed that he says you must pay attention to in order to stay out of trouble. His bill for an additional $4,000 accompanies his report. You are stunned by both the numbers.

People

You decide to seek help elsewhere because you believe you cannot afford extensive startup legal fees. Until you start getting paid for your work on the contract, you need to save your cash on hand to cover payroll and the cash flow requirements of the contract. In addition, you need to buy some new equipment, license some software, and hire two new employees.

Luckily, one of your closest friends works in an aerospace firm as a program manager. You ask him for assistance and he agrees to help you. He looks over the clauses the lawyer itemized and says, "Wow, this seems a little much for so small a contract." He then helps you develop a negotiating strategy that takes the sting out of the government's seemingly unreasonable requirements (at least for a contract of this size). He advises that you plead overkill when you contact the buyer and say that the terms and conditions of the contract that are being proposed are neither fair nor reasonable for a small business SBIR effort.

You contact the government buyer and set up a teleconference. Your friend takes a day off from his job to be at your side when the call is made. The buyer says that because you have no history of performing on a large contract like this one, the risk relative to your performance to the government is high. Therefore, he concludes the terms proposed in the government's offer seem fair and reasonable. You argue that many of these seem like overkill, and the costs associated with putting the necessary systems and procedures in place prior to and during the contract will increase overhead and G&A costs tremendously. He says you will be compensated for these additional costs, if they occur, when the actual overhead and G&A rates are calculated and adjusted to reimburse your actual costs. You argue that these past rates are based on fewer employees and a smaller firm. He holds the line and says that nobody really knows what the rates will be. "Let us wait and see," he argues. "The true rates will be those that actually occur on the job," he states with finality.

You next argue that limiting work to US citizens presents a real hardship because several of your key employees are holders of green cards. He responds by saying they can be authorized to work on the contract as long as they are located in an area of the firm in which classified work is not being performed and informs you that firewalls to separate classified and unclassified work need to be built.

The more that you bring up, the less progress you seem to make. He says to take your list and send it to him with your proposals for resolving any issues associated with the contract, and he will respond to your suggestions within a week. However, the buyer seems neither sympathetic to your pleas nor flexible in his positions when it comes to either your issues or proposed resolutions. Your friend tells you the buyer, after making some minor concessions, is saying you can take the contract or leave it.

Options, recommendations, and reactions

You conclude the teleconference and take action by sending him your list. You and your friend then go out to dinner to discuss what to do next. Your friend suggests that you try to negotiate the more onerous terms and conditions. He agrees to work with you over the weekend to complete this task, which results in the options, recommendations, and the buyer's reactions/responses that are listed in Table 5-1. You need this business to expand the firm. You also have made commitments to your commercial partner that would be embarrassing to back out of. You therefore make the decision to do whatever you need to do in order to get the contract awarded, regardless of concessions you have to make.

TABLE 5-1 Proposed contract options, recommendations, and reactions.

Contract Clause	Options	Recommendations	Reactions
Cost-plus-fixed-fee (CPFF) contract.	Use other type, like fixed-price or labor-hour contract.	Move to a fixed-price-fixed-fee contract like the one used for the Phase I award.	Too much risk; stick with CPFF contract.
Overhead and G&A rates result in 20 percent more hours.	Use different rates that take new hires into account.	Agree to increase rates halfway between what the firm proposed and what the government thinks is reasonable until an audit confirms them.	Too much risk; stick with validated past-performance numbers.
Keep 20 percent of actual costs and profit in reserve until actual rates are fixed.	Keep less of actual costs and profit in reserve per SBIR contract guidelines.	Agree to keep just 10 percent of actual costs and profit in reserve until actual rates are fixed.	Agreed; will comply with SBIR suggested guidelines.
The key personnel clause includes everyone in firm.	Limit key personnel to key performers on the contract.	Limit key personnel to officers and chief engineer.	Agreed, but include project manager as well.
No foreign labor is allowed.	Relax requirements to allow those with valid green cards and visas to work on the contract.	Permit green card holders and those with valid student visas to work on the contract.	Green card holders OK, but students are not because they pose a security risk on the contract.

Contract Clause	Options	Recommendations	Reactions
Intellectual property restrictions.	Government gets limited rights, and your firm gets greater rights to use and market the technology.	That option seems reasonable to your firm's attorney, but make sure that the commercial partner has similar rights to market the technology.	Agreed; standard agreement per terms for an SBIR contract.
Excessive reporting requirements.	Limit reports to what is actually needed to confirm that progress is commensurate with payments on the contract.	Reduce the number of reports proposed to a total that delivers about half the volume of reports included in the contract.	Technical people want these reports, so this request is not approved.
Earned value reporting is required within 60 days of award of contract.	Use another type of progress measurement to provide confidence progress is being made.	Use rate of progress charts to depict project performance. Deliver the charts with the progress reports.	Technical people want earned value reports, so this request is not approved.
Have finance and accounting systems validated.	We are too small a firm to be held to this requirement per current acquisition regulations.	Waive the requirement.	Waived.
Spend 10 percent with minority subcontractors.	We are too small a firm to be held to this requirement per current acquisition regulations.	Waive the requirement.	Waived.
Certify compliance with equal opportunity laws	We are too small a firm to be held to this requirement per current acquisition regulations.	Waive the requirement.	Waived.
Certify compliance with convict labor rules, ball bearing rules, and other such items.	Not applicable for a software R&D contract.	Waive the requirements.	Waived.
Get customer approvals for publications.	Accept.	Accept.	No issue.
Meet security clearance requirements.	Accept.	Accept.	No issue.
Other requirements.	For the most part, the firm accepts, assuming that the requirements are applicable to small firms.	Accept or waive based on the size of the firm.	For the most part, these recommendations are accepted.

Outcomes and lessons learned

You are under contract. It is the third month, and you still have not been paid. Because the government relies on electronic funds transfers, you have had a lot of wickets to go through to get the funds deposited into your account. During the first month, your original invoice was rejected because it did not use the proper forms and procedures. You fixed this promptly after being notified of the problem two weeks after you submitted the invoice. Next, errors in the computation of the amount of money to be withheld caused your invoice to be rejected again. After meeting with the local payment officials, you were able to correct this problem as well. Now, the payment folks are telling you that you need to coordinate payment details with your bank to override the funds transfer that was rejected because accounts were linked improperly. You get cracking on this as soon as you hear about it. Meanwhile, you had to take out a loan to meet payroll because your receivables were not adequate to pay your employees.

Lots of other issues have arisen during startup. The most bothersome of these seems to revolve around the increased costs you are experiencing because of the extra bookkeeping and reporting requirements of the contract. With regard to bookkeeping, the requirements have forced you to implement a job accounting system. Because every contract transaction has to have a job number associated with it, you had to hire your bookkeeper full time to keep up with the seemingly ever increasing bookkeeping workload. You also had to install a new financial system, which cost $7,500 to license the software and $1,500 for training.

Your team is also finding the reporting requirements are overwhelming. They are so busy generating paper that they are finding little time to devote to the prototype software development effort. The customer representative who is providing oversight and direction on the contract says that this is normal. Once you get the paperwork right, he advises, the rest of the job will go really quickly. But the team wants to get done with the paperwork and start coding.

The person who has the biggest load seems to be the project manager. He seems to be on the phone constantly with the customer representative. He is being told to provide this information and prepare this other information for dissemination and presentation to customer management and potential users. In addition, the earned value reports he generated were rejected, as was his first progress report, because neither conformed to the contract's report formats and standards. He fixed the progress report within two days. The earned value reports were more tedious to deal with, and he has to wait for the financial system software to be fully operational before he can even think of trying to submit the required reports. He and your full-time bookkeeper are spending a lot of time on this. You would, however, rather have him focus on the development. Maybe that will be possible once he gets the earned value system up and running. But, based on the paperwork workload and amount of time demanded by the customer, you doubt it.

While these startup challenges seem normal to the customer, the heartburn and expenditures associated with them are not small. The amount of oversight placed on the job and the management burden to keep the customers happy are also much larger than you ever experienced. Although the research effort is interesting and exciting, the amount of red tape and paperwork associated with it are becoming overwhelming.

The lessons learned in this defense-agency, small-business-contract case study were many and include, but are not limited to, the following:

- As this case illustrates, not all change is good. Sometimes the results are other than the desired ones.

- Defense contracts have many requirements that commercial firms are not used to and do not understand. Before entering into a contract, be sure to review the requirements carefully because these can have major impacts on your performance.

- Sometimes it makes sense to not take a job. This is especially true when the change causes too many disturbances and the job diverts resources away from your core competence.[7]

- Small businesses must stress fairness and reasonableness when negotiating contract terms and conditions with government officials. If the terms offered are not reasonable, these firms should fight hard to get them right.

- Small businesses need to focus on performance, not paperwork. This is hard to do on contracts that stress the latter instead of the former.

- If you cannot get the buyer to waive unreasonable contract requirements, try to enlist the support of your customer representative. He may be able to help you get decisions reversed, especially when you can convince him of the merit of your arguments.

- The burden will ease once you tune your systems and procedures to satisfy the government's requirements. Although implementing it can be burdensome, automation can make the change acceptable.

- The next contract will be much easier. The government auditors will know you, and you will know them and what they want. In addition, your systems and procedures will work in a manner acceptable to them and to your customers.

Summary

This chapter provides insights into the challenges associated with requirements imposed by contracts, both government and commercial. The major lessons learned in this case revolve around knowing what the contract says and seeking relief for terms and conditions that do not make sense. Another lesson is to identify non-traditional contract terms that can have major impacts on your contract-related performance. From a change management point of view, altering the way you do business must make business sense and applying change management techniques while doing so is imperative. Otherwise, why make changes? Also, realize that it is always to your advantage to reduce bureaucracy and paperwork. Such efficiencies permit you to focus on getting the work done in the most economical manner possible. In the commercial world, such efficiencies and economies are important and create a marketplace discriminator. For government contracts, they do not seem that important. What is important to them is oversight and insight. That is the reason there is so much paperwork and bureaucracy involved.

References

References cited within this chapter include the following:

[1] Information about the SBIR program can be found at *http://www.sbir.gov*.

[2] Eldad Eilam, *Reversing: Secrets of Reverse Engineering* (Wiley Publishing, 2005).

[3] Department of Defense Defense Contract Audit Agency, *Information for Contractors*, DCAAP 7641.90, January 2005.

[4] John J. Marciniak and Donald J. Reifer, *Software Acquisition Management* (John Wiley & Sons, 1990).

[5] Information on green cards is accessible from the following government website: *http://www.uscis. gov/portal/site/uscis/menuitem.eb1d4c2a3e5b9ac89243c6a7543f6d1a/?vgnextoid=ae853ad15c6732 10VgnVCM100000082ca60aRCRD&vgnextchannel=ae853ad15c673210VgnVCM100000082ca60aR CRD*.

[6] Quentin W. Fleming and Joel M. Koffleman, *Earned Value Project Management*, 4th ed. (Project Management Institute, 2010).

[7] C. K. Prahalad and Gary Hamel, "The Core Competence of the Corporation," *Harvard Business Review*, Boston, MA, May-June 1990.

Web resources

Applicable web resources that amplify points made in this chapter can be found here:

- The Data & Analysis Center for Software (DACS) provides lots of resources to help with software acquisition management issues at *http://www.thedacs.com*.

- The Software Engineering Institute (SEI) developed the CMMI for Acquisition (CMMI-ACQ), which is available, along with other acquisition resources, at *http://www.sei.cmu.edu/cmmi/ solutions/acq/*. The SEI previously developed a Software Acquisition Capability Maturity Model in 2002. The model is available at *http://www.sei.cmu.edu/reports/02tr010.pdf*.

- An excellent set of guidelines on software acquisition management, including those involving small businesses, can be found in a guidebook published by the Defense Contract Management Agency (DCMA) at the following site: *http://guidebook.dcma.mil/55/index.cfm*.

- A good case study highlighting successful acquisition management practices can be found at *http://www.intfedsol.com/documents/Case%20Study%20-%20Web%20Based%20Acquisition%20Management.pdf*.

- The Department of Defense (DOD) maintains an earned value website with tutorials, newsletters, and other resources at *http://www.acq.osd.mil/pm*.

- Defense Acquisition University educates and trains the DOD's acquisition workforce and provides career-long training via the programs described at *http://www.dau.mil/Training/default.aspx*.

- American Graduate University has a School of Acquisition Management that offers degrees, certificates, and training in related subject areas, which is described at *http://www.agu.edu/Acquisition_mgnt/master_acquisition.html*.

- Defense Acquisition University also conducts conferences on acquisition management that bring together the community to discuss topics of interest. The link to their current conferences is available at *http://www.dau.mil/images/Pages/Conferences.aspx*.

CHAPTER 6

Industrial Case: Utility Moving to the Clouds

Setting the stage

The utility company you work for is considering moving to cloud computing. Cloud computing, as you find out via the Internet, is a relatively new concept that refers to an assortment of logical computational resources that are made available via computer networks rather than on local computers.[1,2] Applications are hosted on multiple servers across the cloud. Data is also stored on server farms. In this manner, both applications and data can be made accessible via a browser rather than you having to install and run them on your desktop, laptop, or office server. Instead, both run on the cloud via its servers and results are made available through the network to clients on their computers. Clouds can be public and private, depending on the need. In addition, cloud services are sold on a demand basis using any of these three arrangements:

- **Software as a service**   End-user applications services are accessed over the network rather than on client computers. Under this arrangement, you execute your business application remotely to get results typically at a fraction of the cost of licensing the software.

- **Platform as a service**   Sets of application components can be put together by developers via plug-and-play and run on cloud-computing servers to get results.

- **Infrastructure as a service**   Developers can build applications from scratch and run them in virtual machines on the cloud servers without having to license tooling that can be costly.

The major advantage of cloud computing is its significantly lower cost relative to the older model, where you would acquire and maintain hardware and software resources. It removes the need for large capital investments in equipment, infrastructure, and software and reduces related operating costs proportionately. It also increases potential mobility because the only thing workers need to do, wherever they are, to access computational resources is connect to the cloud.

The disadvantages of cloud computing are many and include becoming dependent on someone else to control your computational resources. As a consequence, you will fail if they do or if they are unwilling to pitch in to resolve a crisis. Besides other disadvantages, the cloud has serious security and privacy risks, especially if confidential data is not protected adequately. Obviously, there is lots of information available about cloud computing in the professional literature[3,4] and on the Internet. (See the end of this chapter for pointers to these resources.)

Your task in this case study is to lead an internal team that has been asked by management to determine whether or not to use cloud computing to provide basic services for your firm and its customers. Customers are residential, industrial, and governmental users of the gas, power, energy, water, and waste-removal services that your firm offers on a fee-for-service basis throughout the municipality.

Organization

Figure 6-1 shows an organizational chart of the entire utility company.

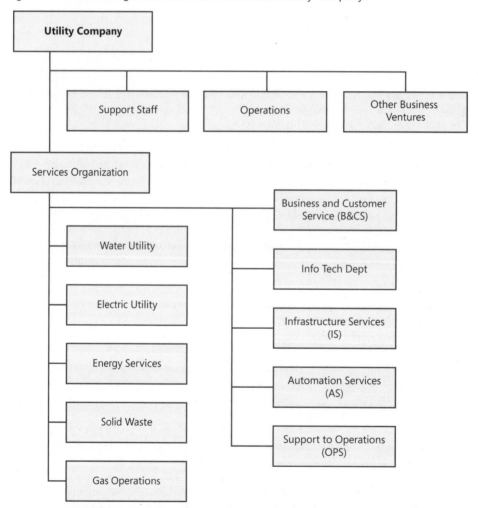

FIGURE 6-1 Organizational chart for the utility company.

The part of the company you are most interested in is the Services organization, which provides a wide range of utility services for a large city and its suburbs. The Information Technology (IT) department of which you are a part provides centralized support for each of these groups from the company's main offices located in a large city in the southern United States. The department provides infrastructure services for the enterprise as a whole, and automation and operations support services for each of the groups that are part of the Services organization. In addition, IT has a major field site co-located with the services group's Business and Customer Service (B&CS) organization, which is about 30 miles away. This field site was built as a backup for the main site in case a disaster occurs. Both sites have development facilities and service the firm's client/server networks. The IT department has 1,200 professionals located at these sites and 300 support personnel. The IT general manager also serves as the chief information officer (CIO) of the company. However, the vice president of operations is responsible for ensuring that the services provided by operations personnel is exemplary at the many sites the company maintains across the country in cities, counties, and government facilities.

Project

The project you are in charge of is primarily tasked with determining whether or not to use cloud computing within the IT department to lower operating costs for infrastructure services like payroll and travel. You have a team of three who are working with you part time to develop a recommendation regarding the use of what management views as a beneficial, cost-cutting technology.

During your team's kickoff meeting, the IT general manager provides the following added information and direction for the effort:

- Assess whether moving to cloud computing makes sense for B&CS and Infrastructure Services (IS) because they each maintain various resources that other groups access via the company's client-server network. The capital assets of each group (equipment, licenses, and other items) are listed in Table 6-1.

- The number of staff currently required to operate and maintain B&CS and IS facilities and equipment is listed in Table 6-2. These counts address common software used across the company. They do not include the staff used to develop new software applications, who are funded separately by the operational groups.

- Determine the impact of cloud computing on the IT department's capital costs of doing business. As part of this analysis, look at what happens to the equipment and facilities that will be disposed of when the department transitions to the use of cloud computing.

- Make sure that no matter what you do the same quality of service (or better service) is provided to your customers. This is determined by using the current primary measure, which assesses response time relative to a customer's request for service.

- Retain any applications that provide the company with clear advantages over the competition, such as the company's current ability to read meters remotely to tabulate billings.

- Investigate how to address the security and privacy shortfalls of cloud computing. Make sure customer proprietary information is protected regardless of the cost.

TABLE 6-1 Capital assessment for the B&CS and IS groups.

Organization	Asset	Purchase Price (in millions)	Accumulated Depreciation[b] (in millions)	Current Book Value (in millions)
B&CS	Computer equipment	$40	$20	$20
	Communications gear	15	8	7
	Software licenses	20	7	13
	Capital improvements[a]	25	10	15
	TOTALS	**$100**	**$45**	**$55**
IS	Computer equipment	$60	$25	$35
	Communications gear	20	10	10
	Software licenses	20	8	12
	Capital improvements[a]	50	22	28
	TOTALS	**$150**	**$65**	**$85**

[a] Expenses to improve leased facilities (long term)

[b] Using IRS guidelines for depreciation for different types of equipment and licenses

TABLE 6-2 Annual average staff expenses to maintain and operate computational resources.

Organization	Task	Annual Cost (in millions)[a]
B&CS	Hardware and software maintenance	$2
	Sustaining engineering, including user support	2
	Operational support (includes call center)	4
	Product management	1
	TOTALS	**$9 (45 people)**
IS	Hardware and software maintenance	$5
	Sustaining engineering, including user support	2
	Operational support	2
	Product management	1
	TOTALS	**$10 (50 people)**

[a] Cost for a staff-year of effort is assumed to be $200,000 at this price level.

Process

The approach your team decides to take to make your determinations and findings adheres to the practice your firm has in place for such analyses. The steps are outlined as follows:

- **Step 1: Develop a Concept Paper**   Summarize your concept of operations in a white paper for cloud computing use in B&CS, and summarize its use in IS in a white paper that highlights the capabilities you hope to acquire from the vendors.

- **Step 2: Issue a Public Request for Information**   Issue a public Request for Information (RFI) asking vendors to comment on your white paper and tell you how they would go about satisfying its requirements.

- **Step 3: Gather Information/Develop Requirements**   Hold discussions with vendors who provide technically acceptable responses to the list of items you asked them to address in your white paper. These include the evaluation criteria you identified in the paper to be used to make such determinations and findings.

- **Step 4: Prepare/Issue a Request for Proposal (RFP)**   Issue an RFP to vendors who responded to your RFI for the acquisition of cloud-computing systems and services based on a solicitation that contains your requirements, work statement, and preferred contractual terms and conditions. Make sure that your solicitation does not bias the acquisition by using vendor proprietary information gathered via the RFI process. Otherwise, you might have to deal with a protest from one of the losing vendors.

- **Step 5: Conduct Source Evaluation/Selection**   Using criteria (responsive to requirements, lowest cost, minimum risk, and other such items) contained within the solicitation, rate and rank the vendor proposals. Make a selection based on the given criteria. Identify major strengths and weaknesses in the winning proposal, and forward it along with your recommendations to those responsible for negotiating a contract.

- **Step 6: Issue a Contract**   Negotiate with the selected vendor to acquire the products and services using best value and fairness as your overriding principles. Work with the vendor to take advantage of its strengths and compensate for its weaknesses. Remember, the vendor must succeed for you to succeed.

- **Step 7: Monitor the Contractor/Accept Delivery**   Provide oversight and direction as the contractor works to comply with your requirements for delivery of acceptable products and services. Accept delivery only when the vendor supplies evidence of compliance with your contract requirements.

- **Step 8: Commence Operations**   Using your concept of operations, transition to the use of the cloud-computing products and services acquired in as disciplined, logical, and risk-free a manner as possible. Apply change-management principles during the transition. Remember to plan in detail because the transition might require you to operate systems in parallel to minimize potential impacts when running a shop 24 hours a day/7 days a week. Be sure to include recurring activities, such as maintaining ongoing communications with stakeholders.

The response to the RFI is overwhelming. You received 42 replies, of which 18 vendors seem to satisfy your requirements. In addition, the telephone has not been idle for the past two days. Most of these phone calls are vendors asking for time to visit and present their wares to you and your team. However, your timeline will not accommodate them all. You need to cut the number to six vendors, at most. You do this by asking all of those responding if they have experience with utility companies similar to yours. Because only three of the six can respond positively, you can reduce the list of promising vendors accordingly.

Product

After discussions with the vendors, you feel that you have the information you need to pull together a briefing to your boss and his staff on how to exploit the use of cloud computing within your utility company. Your briefing will contain the following observations and recommendations relative to the changeover:

- The move to private cloud computing, where facilities are dedicated to the company, has many benefits as confirmed by government studies[5,6] and all of the vendor sales pitches. Costs can be substantially reduced, and the company's ability to expand and contract its computing resources as needed is greatly enhanced.

- Given the current business picture and constrained B&CS and IS budgets, private cloud computing seems to represent a viable path forward for the utility.

- The ability to implement a measured service under a pay-for-use paradigm, which provides services on an on-demand basis across a ubiquitous network, has many advantages.

- All those interviewed concurred that private cloud computing seems to make the most sense for IS because the services it provides are for the entire organization. Because B&CS is localized, it does not seem to make sense to use private clouds for them on a broader basis.

- Cost savings will be realized as a function of the substitution of virtualized applications software in the cloud for labor and facilities from current dedicated resources.

- Cost savings from the cloud can be realized in stages as various applications are replaced by vendor replacements. Transition to private cloud computing will outsource general business applications first and then operations and maintenance later.

- The team recommends going forward with private clouds for IS but not for B&CS. The next steps in the process will pull together the requirements, develop a solicitation, and issue an RFP for the acquisition of products and services.

- In preparing for the RFP, the team will identify and seek to retain core services that are fundamental to the way the utility does business and that represent a competitive advantage, such as the ability to read meters remotely and bill clients directly for services, as mentioned earlier.

- In the RFP, current systems will be kept operational and working in parallel during a transition period of three to five years. Some business process reengineering will be required during the transition to optimize how the new cloud-computing resources are used.

- In the RFP, as a risk mitigation action, those proposing solutions will be asked how they can address known weaknesses of cloud computing, such as those related to security and privacy.

- In the RFP, purchase and maintenance options will be included to provide the utility with leverage once the acquisition is completed and the vendor is under contract.

People

Your boss liked your briefing, nodded his head in agreement many times as he listened, and concurred when you concluded with all of your team's recommendations. However, the head of IS was infuriated and vocally criticized every one of your charts. Such protests were expected because IS would be taking the brunt of the cuts. When you were asked how much could be saved, you replied, "Based on vendor inputs during the question and answer sessions, they estimated savings between $50 and $60 million of equipment at book value and from 35 to 40 people with a total staff cost between $7 and $8 million. The total reduction based on these numbers is between $57 and $68 million from the current budget of $95 million."

The head of IS immediately responds to these numbers with a blistering rebuttal. He states that such savings are unrealistic because much of this equipment and the people will have to be retained to run existing facilities in parallel during the three-to-five-year transition period. In addition, at least five new people will have to be hired during this period to perform the business process reengineering tasks, including the staff needed to train users in their proper utilization. He estimates that the conversion costs during the three to five years will add $8 to $10 million to IS's current operating expenses. These numbers rattle you, the general manager, and the audience. "He is right," says the general manager. "You need to investigate the costs of transition more fully before I make a go/no-go decision on the acquisition," he continues.

The head of IS has a grin on his face and looks pleased. He volunteers to have two of his best senior people work with you part time as you develop a response. You politely decline, but the general manager thinks it is a good idea, and you reluctantly accept the offer of help. The general manager schedules an additional meeting two weeks from this one to review the cloud-computing recommendations again.

You should have expected and prepared for the IS response because anticipating and planning for resistance is a fundamental change-management principle. But you did not. Getting cloud computing accepted now will be harder. But it still seems doable.

Options, recommendations, and reactions

The team gets together to assess the options with the transition in mind. They identify the following four main transition scenarios to cloud computing that everyone agrees make sense:

- **Option 1: General Application-Only Transition**   Transition most general applications to a private cloud, retain IS facilities and staff to run general applications, and continue servicing customers on a fee-for-service basis.

- **Option 2: Partial Facilities Transition + Option 1**   Perform Option 1, and shut down unneeded facilities within IS. Sell off equipment, and reduce staff proportionately as private cloud services and applications become operational. Upgrade equipment as needed to address reliability issues.

- **Option 3: Transition to Upgraded Facilities + Fuller Set of Applications**   During the transition to the private cloud, upgrade facilities to provide core processing and backup. Address current equipment reliability issues that are occurring as gear ages and failures increase, thus jeopardizing 24/7 operations. Sell off equipment, and adjust staff proportionately as facilities and cloud services and applications become operational.

- **Option 4: Operate IS As-Is**   Upgrade IS equipment to address reliability problems, and continue to operate as-is. Perform some streamlining to cut costs and improve service to consumers.

Table 6-3 summarizes the results of the team's analyses after considerable debate. It identifies the major strengths and weaknesses of each option, along with the estimated costs and projected benefits. The table seems to highlight the overall conclusion that movement to one of the three private cloud-computing options is the right thing to do even though IS remains reluctant to support such a recommendation (that is, the two people assigned to your team neither concurred with this analysis nor agreed to put their names on the results).

TABLE 6-3 Strengths and weaknesses of cloud-computing options.

Options	Strength	Weakness	Cost	Benefits
General Applications Only in Clouds	■ Big gains, little effort ■ Can handle increased workloads ■ Minimal disturbance	■ Does not address the reliability issue	■ Transition cost of $25 million ■ Two to three years before benefits accrue	■ Cost avoidance of $40 million a year ■ Increased flexibility ■ Can handle a larger workload
Partial Facilities + Partial Applications in Clouds	■ Improve ability to respond quickly as business conditions change via the cloud ■ Addresses reliability issues	■ Transition is hard and takes time ■ New jobs must be found for displaced staff ■ Business processes must be updated	■ Transition cost of $50 million ■ Three to five years before benefits accrue	■ Cost avoidance of $50 million a year ■ Better business processes ■ Reliability issues handled ■ Less equipment and staff to worry about
Upgrade Facilities + Fuller Set of Applications in Clouds	■ Same strengths as Option 2 plus company can back up clouds with its own facilities	■ Same weaknesses of Option 2 plus more turmoil during transition	■ Transition cost of $65 million ■ Three to five years before benefits accrue	■ Cost avoidance of $65 million a year ■ All the benefits listed previously
Operate IS As-Is	■ Minimum pain	■ Minimum gain	■ Minimum cost	■ Reliability issue is addressed

Outcomes and lessons learned

Your next meeting with the IT general manager and the head of Infrastructure Services is stormy. It is apparent during the meeting that the head of IS is unhappy with the results. He continuously bombards you during your briefing with nasty remarks, and he accuses you several times of deliberately ignoring his people's inputs. In addition, he blasts the legitimacy of the numbers and asks for details on how each was derived. You respond with the spreadsheets that provide backup and tell him that his own people reviewed the numbers and found them reasonable.

Your boss finally has no option but to tell everyone to cool down. He states that even though the numbers speak for themselves and seem to present a solid business case for change, he has concerns. His major trepidations, he says, are the risks associated with the transition and the displacement of personnel. He says that equipment has to be changed no matter what option is chosen because it is wearing out and the reliability declines have to be fixed. Based on his remarks, it is not surprising that he accepts Option 2. In response, you and your team take the action to move to the next step in the process by preparing and issuing an RFP. You hope that several of the vendors who replied to your RFI will respond to your RFP with proposals that provide good value for your money.

Your team meets and tries to scope what goes into the RFP besides the requirements and boilerplate text. A member of your team who has been through a large purchase like this before advises you to pay attention to the boilerplate text because this is where the evaluation criteria for selection and the terms and conditions for the purchase go. That's good advice, you think. So you schedule a meeting between your team and the Purchasing staff.

The meeting with the Purchasing staff goes very well. They had lots of experience and advice about what to put in the solicitation document. Key provisions include rewards for delivering early and penalties for being late. They also provide options to acquire several products and services (additional applications and services, more equipment, training, and other such items) that can be taken after the contract is awarded at a fixed price. Maintenance terms and conditions for the first five years of operations were also spelled out so that you can get the vendor's immediate and undivided attention when problems occur after delivery.

At the suggestion of the Purchasing department, you send the solicitation out to the prospective suppliers for comment prior to releasing it. You get back a lot of constructive criticism and suggestions. You find that the most controversial clauses are those associated with late delivery and maintenance.

The lessons learned in this industrial case study were many and include, but are not limited to, the following:

- Even when you think there is a clear choice, resistance to change can pop up from unexpected sources. Therefore, also anticipate resistance and plan to deal with it.

- Resistance to change comes primarily from those whose power, staff, and budgets are threatened. In this case, such cutbacks are real threats to the Infrastructure Services group.

- Those who foster change need to anticipate the perceived threats and develop plans to help address them as part of their effort. In this case, figuring out how to find other positions for staff who are no longer needed might have alleviated some of the pain.

- There might be hidden issues that influence decisions relative to change. In this case, aging equipment and reliability issues did not surface until late in the process when options were being compared. Yet, the issue was one of the major drivers in determining which option was selected.

- Using competitive market forces to seek the best alternative can be beneficial, especially if you can get an expert review of your solicitation by stimulating the vendors to provide you inputs as to which of your requirements are feasible and which are not.

- However, relying solely on vendor inputs is dangerous. Because they want to make a sale, they might stretch facts and cloud reality by confusing current capabilities with future capabilities.

- Using strengths and weaknesses along with costs and benefits permits stronger cases to be made for recommended alternatives.

- Getting a vendor on contract takes considerable time and effort. It also forces you to solidify your concepts of operations, requirements, and contract terms and conditions.

- Getting selected vendors to deliver what they promise often takes patience, effort, and due diligence. Many will do a good job. Others may let you down after the contract is issued. To succeed, plan to manage rather than monitor the contract. Otherwise, you probably will get less than what you expect and less than what you are paying for.

- The challenge will occur after the cloud products and services are delivered and accepted. If you are not one of the vendor's key accounts, keeping their attention during operations and maintenance might become an issue. That is why I strongly recommend negotiating terms and conditions for any follow-on maintenance contract as part of the original acquisition.

Summary

This chapter provides insight into large procurements for Information Technology (IT) products and services. The major issues in this case revolve around addressing resistance to change brought on by a changeover to a new computing paradigm—for example, cloud computing. In this case, such resistance should have been anticipated and dealt with earlier in the process. The team should have gotten IS personnel involved earlier and solicited their inputs and resolved their objections prior to making the recommendation for one of the change options. In the process, they would have learned about and been able to attack the issues of reliability and placement of staff. Instead, they became involved in a war of words that detracted from the goal of the effort, which was determining whether or not cloud computing made sense for this utility company.

This is another chapter where I cut back on materials to save space and maintain a focus. Please understand that cloud computing is controversial and has many issues associated with it that deserve further coverage. For example, the performance of the cloud is overstated—that is, the vendor often promises more performance at a lower cost than it can deliver. As another example, the tools you use may or may not work as advertised on the cloud. Be warned that you need to move carefully to the clouds because they are still in their early-adopter period.

References

References cited within this chapter include the following:

[1] Charles Babcock, "Why Private Cloud Computing Is Real—And Worth Considering," *Information-Week*, April 11, 2009.

[2] Amazon web services provides numerous case studies on cloud computing at the following site: *http://aws.amazon.com/solutions/case-studies*.

[3] The Cloud Computing Journal has published numerous success stories that can be reviewed at *http://cloudcomputing.sys-con.com/node/1687873*.

[4] Marc Benioff and Carlye Adler, *Behind the Cloud: The Untold Story of How Salesforce.com Went from Idea to Billion-Dollar Company and Revolutionized an Industry* (Jossey-Bass, 2009).

[5] Government Computer News devoted an entire issue of the magazine in 2011 to cloud computing successes that is accessible at *http://gcn.com/microsites/2011/cloud-computing-snapshot/index.aspx*.

[6] NASA Nebula Project. Information about their use of cloud computing is available at the following site: *http://nebula.nasa.gov*.

Web resources

Applicable web resources that amplify points made in this chapter can be found here:

- Amazon has many books and articles on the subject of cloud computing. Go to *http://www.amazon.com* to find relevant publications.

- Amazon also provides infrastructure web services via a cloud platform for commercial companies of all sizes via a fee-for-service arrangement for application hosting, backup and storage, e-commerce, media hosting, search engines, web hosting, and other services.

- YouTube has a number of videos on cloud computing, like the following one that introduces you to the technology: *http://www.youtube.com/watch?v=ae_DKNwK_ms*.

- Many technology firms in the cloud-computing business provide resources to help those investigating this technology. For example, Hewlett-Packard offers a planning guide at its cloud-computing digital hub at *http://www.techlearning.com/article.aspx?Id=39248*.

- The Open Cloud Consortium (OCC) manages cloud computing resources and develops reference implementations, benchmarks, and standards for its members that support scientific research. Information about the consortium is available at *http://opencloudconsortium.org/about*.

■ IBM and the European Union have announced the formation of a consortium to research new computing models. See *http://www-03.ibm.com/press/us/en/pressrelease/33067.wss*.

■ The Cloud Computing Journal offers lots of articles on the use of the technology at *http://cloudcomputing.sys-con.com*.

■ Another useful publication called the Cloudbook, located at the following site, provides relevant articles: *http://www.cloudbook.net*.

■ Lots of technology firms, training companies, and universities offer training in cloud-computing areas.

■ Major conferences and expositions on cloud computing such as the following are held in large cities worldwide: *http://www.interop.com/newyork/conference/cloud-computing.php*.

■ A current list of cloud-computing discussion groups, list servers, and blogs can be found at *http://www.thedacs.com/databases/url/key/7848/7852*.

■ A nonprofit group of major technology firms has been formed to address cloud-computing security issues. It is called the Cloud Security Alliance, and it has many resources at the following site: *https://cloudsecurityalliance.org*.

CHAPTER 7

Industrial Case: Adoption of Agile Methods

Setting the stage

You work for a firm that develops popular software development tools and tool systems that are sold commercially. The wide variety and types of tools being marketed include the following:

- Browsers

- Compilers

- Cost models

- Debuggers

- Dynamic analyzers

- Metrics analyzers

- Performance analyzers

- Regression test managers

- Standards enforcers

- Static analyzers

- Test managers

- Text editors

- Version control packages

These tools are state of the art and very popular with techies because they automate a wide range of functions they perform when developing software, provide tool system capabilities, operate on the popular platforms, are compatible with the programming languages, and support your organization's consulting group, which provides the services listed in Table 7-1. The tool systems sold use a common intermediate representation, a data model, and a repository to store the work in progress. Several partners who sell other popular software tools have developed interfaces to bridge their results to and from your repository using the representation and data model noted.

TABLE 7-1 Tool system capabilities, platforms, languages, and services.

Category	Offerings
Tool System Capabilities	■ Build management ■ Configuration management ■ Database management ■ Distribution management ■ Project management ■ Repository management ■ Others
Supported Platforms	Operating Systems: ■ AmigaOS ■ FreeBSD, NetBSD, and others ■ Linux, Unix ■ Mac OS X ■ Microsoft Windows ■ OS2 ■ Solaris ■ Others Frameworks: ■ Adobe Air ■ Java, JDK, and JRE ■ Mono ■ .NET Framework ■ ORACLE database ■ Steam ■ Others
Software Languages	■ C, C++, and C# ■ HTML ■ Java and Java J2EE ■ Perl ■ PHP ■ Python ■ Ruby ■ Visual Basic ■ Visual C++ ■ Others
Services to Be Offered	■ Consulting ■ Education and training ■ Mentoring ■ User support

As the table illustrates, your firm offers an extensive list of software-development-tool products and services. That is why your company is viewed by many as one of the market leaders in the tool business area. However, the area of security is a noticeable hole in your current portfolio that you have been tasked with filling. Based on a market analysis conducted by your sales organization, you need to bring some of the products and services listed in Table 7-2 to market to stay competitive.

TABLE 7-2 Security tools and services to be developed.

Security Tools	Security Services
Dashboard for portraying security assessment results graphically, along with a rating of the relative strength of your protection	Consulting in the area of security
Database auditing tools	Penetration testing
Port scanner	Security assessment
Security analyzer	Security training and mentoring
Vulnerability analyzer	Vulnerability assessment

Note: Interfaces between your tool system and tools developed by others that provide firewall, intrusion-detection, and virus-analysis capabilities

Organization

Your task is to marshal the forces necessary to develop a software-security product line for sale as part of your company's current product and service offerings. You have been pulled out of product development to provide recommendations directly to senior management including the CEO. Money is no object, but time is of the essence. Marketing says that it needs to announce the security push and have an initial product offering available at the upcoming industry trade show in the spring. Their rationale is that your primary competitors will make similar announcements and your firm will lose market share unless it responds aggressively. The CEO and other senior managers of the firm agree with this assessment. Everyone is on the bandwagon but you. You argue that not much can be produced between now and then because the show is just nine months away. They respond by telling you to do your best. However, expectations are raised that you will be able to bring at least one or two products to market within the time period. You feel that your job depends on it.

You determine what resources are available. As highlighted in the organizational chart pictured in Figure 7-1, you have teams in San Francisco, California and Vancouver, British Columbia (Canada) that you can use for the development. The Canadian team comes with an advantage. They have been using Agile methods effectively to develop bindings for integrating partner tools into your software tool system for the past five years. Although these developments have been relatively small (teams of three to five people), the teams have delivered quality products to market much quicker than expected. Based on their positive results, you have high hopes that you can scale the version of the methods they employed for use on your larger security initiative.

You call a meeting of the leads and ask the Vancouver team to brief attendees on their methodology. Figure 7-2 summarizes the key principles and practices that they use for software development. The principles form what has been called the "Manifesto for Agile Software Development."[1] Of course, everyone has lots of questions, all of which are aimed at assessing how easy it will be to learn and use the approach. Many of the practices that the Canadians used were heavily criticized as hobby-shop oriented. There was lots of discussion about which Agile method to use. However, no consensus was reached at the meeting because much of what was debated was based on conjecture rather than actual experience or results.

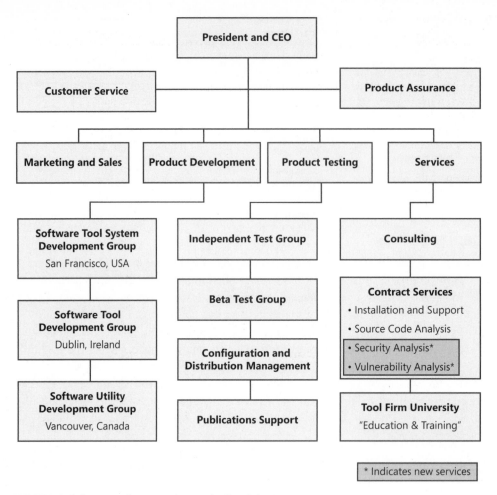

FIGURE 7-1 Software tool company's organizational chart.

Because the firm lets the project lead make the call regarding the development approach, you buy into the approach used by the Canadian team and convince everyone present to agree to use it. Everyone agrees because the Agile approach seems the only way possible to deliver the requested security products and services according to the aggressive schedule. However, you want to pin down the techniques you will use before you venture forth. In response, you enroll in a week-long Agile development course and read all that you can on the use of the techniques. The major criticism you have heard about Agile methods is that they are difficult to apply and do not scale well on larger software development projects.[2] Because you have been given a team of 40 professionals in San Francisco and Vancouver to develop security products and services, you have concerns regarding what practices you should and should not use on this important project.

Principles	Practices	Variants
• Individuals and inter-actions over processes and tools • Working software over comprehensive documentation • Customer collaboration over contract negotiation • Responding to change over following a plan	• Capture requirements via user stories[3] • Form self-organizing teams • Plan iteratively at beginning of each iteration • Deliver frequently—daily builds preferred • Plan to learn—welcome changing requirements throughout the project • Emphasize simplicity in architecture and design • Test everything • Communicate powerfully at daily standup meeting • Measure value—working software is primary measure of progress	• The customer should always be available • Refactor whatever and whenever possible[4] • All production code should be pair programmed[5] • Unit code first (test first)[6] • Emphasize collective ownership of the code—anyone can change it anytime • Move people around • Set a sustainable pace and use velocity as your main measure of progress[7]

FIGURE 7-2 Key principles and practices of Agile methods used by the Canadian team.

Project

You really enjoyed your training course. It confirmed that Agile has merit. But the course you took identified so much to do that you just do not know where to start. You have neither the time nor the luxury to do things wrong the first time around. So you decide to bring in outside professionals to help you.

The firm you hire suggests that you do three things during the next two weeks as you start up the project. First, pin down your delivery requirements by having marketing assemble a representative group of users. Marketing says that user stories will work, especially if they focus on defining desired features/functions lists and performance expectations. Next, have team members define a simple Agile process with a common vocabulary for use by the project. Third and finally, have the team define organizational roles and cross-functional communications paths to keep everyone informed.

Luckily, your team is currently just 12 professionals. More people will join the team every week as it builds to its full quota of 20 in San Francisco and 10 in Vancouver. You will actually have 40 people on the team because 10 other support people, primarily in San Francisco, will be doing version control, quality assurance, and testing tasks. You are trying to persuade marketing to get a couple of security user representatives assigned to your team as well. However, it seems the best you can do is get one internal person assigned to play this role. Luckily, this person has lots of related experience, and you believe he can perform this job almost as well as an outsider.

Process

You can have your team develop its schedule once they are trained in Agile methods and the requirements and organization are put into place. Your experts advise against doing this all at once at the beginning of the project. People forget what they do not use, they advise. Instead, they recommend that training in the methods be done on a just-in-time basis. You agree and schedule an introductory course for the entire team in San Francisco. Your goal is to use the course to get everyone speaking a common Agile vocabulary. You also want the team to focus on defining its cadence once the course is completed based on working product increments that will be released on, at most, a six-week cycle, as illustrated in Figure 7-3. You plan to use velocity as your primary measure to ensure the end game can be realized.

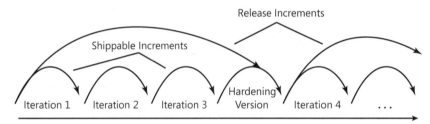

FIGURE 7-3 Conceptual development cadence for the development effort.

Product

The team gathered as a group and accomplished the tasks you laid out for them in an open work area that you acquired for that purpose. First, they consulted with the user representative to define the requirements employing user stories. The results were better than expected. The team was able to come up with usage scenarios and feature lists for the candidate tools rather easily. In addition, the scenarios were easily mapped to services you hope to sell. Using the easiest-out-first approach, the team next established the priorities and target delivery dates for their product and service developments, which are summarized in Table 7-3. The team embraced this approach because it would allow them to generate an initial set of security products and services quickly according to their tight schedule. Note that a penetration test tool was added to the list because the team felt it would be needed to manage the large number of test activities that would be conducted as part of the related service.

TABLE 7-3 Security products and services priorities.

Security Tools	Ease of Development	Priority	Target Delivery Date
Dashboard[a]	Easy	1	9 months
Database auditing tools	Easy	1	9 months
Port scanner[b]	Easy	1	9 months
Security analyzer	Difficult	3	15 months
Penetration test system	Difficult	2	12 months
Vulnerability analyzer[c]	Moderate	1	9 months
Security Services			
Consulting	Easy	1	9 months
Penetration testing	Difficult	2	12 months
Security assessment	Difficult	3	15 months
Security training and mentoring	Moderate	1	Phased starting in 9 months
Vulnerability analysis	Moderate	1	9 months

[a] Dashboard needed in initial delivery to invoke tools and coordinate their activities

[b] Will license scanner from commercial vendor instead of developing it

[c] Tool needed to run vulnerability analyses

One of the tenets of Agile practice is to develop using a well-defined set of coding standards. As part of its kickoff activities, the team agrees to use the C# programming language and the set of design and coding standards that the Canadian group in Vancouver developed because they are very comprehensive. In addition, several members of the team volunteer to draft a life-cycle guide for the process you will use and a set of definitions for the terms being employed. Roles and responsibilities for the group is the last item covered at the meeting. Both groups agree on the tasks that each will be held accountable for, and the support staff agrees to ready a set of blogs for sharing information on their web portal. They will also set up a number of working directories and provide access to everyone on the team.

People

It's clear that people are excited to be members of the team. Every member of the team is putting their all into the effort. Many are working extra hours to read up on Agile methods and get their individual tasks done. As part of the effort, you have embraced the notions of self-organizing teams and daily stand-up meetings. Both are working well. Six teams of six have formed, each selecting its own leader and each generating its own schedule. A seventh team works on integration and infrastructure issues. All of the teams are coordinating their activities and deliveries at the daily stand-up meetings. The overall schedule is posted in the open area you have secured, which has been decorated with white boards. Sticky notes are used to communicate information. The entire space has been virtualized via web cameras so that team members can view the daily proceedings remotely on their personal computers. This makes it possible for the Canadians to be included seamlessly in the operations.

During the early months, the initial product and service iterations have been coming fast and furiously. Some say the reason for all the hustle and bustle is the Hawthorne effect.[8] Others explain it differently. Management bluntly does not care why it is happening. All they care about is product, and it is seemingly being produced at a blistering pace. However, Agile development takes some getting used to for newbies. Although there is product, it has limited functionality. This is expected because the approach used is to develop the architecture first and then add functionality iteration by iteration. You also must get used to performance issues that crop up frequently in the early iterations. But in Agile developments, performance will be enhanced incrementally as refactoring takes place and user expectations are crystalized through constant interaction with the user representative. Everything looks good so far, and management is pleased with the effort. Because of this, they have left the team alone. So has marketing, which has been directing its attention to key accounts. They are busy letting these accountholders know about the new product and service offerings. What is on their minds is sales, not status. This makes everyone's life simpler.

Options, recommendations, and reactions

It has been six months and there has been lots of activity, but little perceived progress on the development effort. Although there has been a working product for months, it is neither in a state where it can be demonstrated nor in a state where it can be sold. Worse yet, marketing and management have lost their confidence in the team. They ask questions and get told to basically "Trust me." Becoming nervous, they are starting to make demands that are causing the team to lose focus.

Things come to a head when the next iteration is delivered. The dashboard, port scanner, and database analyzer are included, but the vulnerability analyzer is not. Because it is the showpiece of the security toolset offering, concern is raised. The team in San Francisco developing it says that they are 90 percent complete with the first version and it will be delivered as part of the next iteration in six weeks. However, it is mid-November and everyone knows from experience that little gets done between November and New Year's Day because of the holidays.

Because of its current lack of confidence in the team's ability to deliver, marketing pesters management into scheduling a project review during the next week. Both marketing and management want to take stock of where the project is in development, identify issues, and do whatever is deemed necessary to ensure delivery occurs as promised for the upcoming show.

You hold a meeting with all of your leads later that afternoon to decide what information you will present at the review. Of course, you will present the current status of development as summarized in Table 7-4. But you also decide to build confidence by summarizing some of the key wins, as listed in Table 7-5, since the rollout of the Agile methodology began.

One of the primary reasons why things have not gone according to plan according to your leads is that the security knowledge they need in order to be successful is not readily available. Experts are reluctant to talk about security issues, and there are no compilations that provide the knowledge your people seek in order to get the products ready for the marketplace. Solutions suggested during your discussions with others on how to fix the problem include buying or partnering with a firm that can provide you with this knowledge.

TABLE 7-4 Current status of the security tool suite development at month 6.

Security Tools	Current Status	Target Delivery	Anticipated Delivery
Dashboard[a]	Fully functional. Testing will be completed in the next iteration. Refactoring is under way.	9 months	7 months
Database auditing tools	Fully functional. Testing will be completed in the next iteration. Refactoring is under way.	9 months	7 months
Port scanner[b]	Fully functional. Testing will be completed in the next iteration. Refactoring is under way.	9 months	7 months
Security analyzer	The plug-in has been developed with minimal functionality. The process of defining the operational scenario has started.	15 months	15 months
Penetration test system	The plug-in has been developed with minimal functionality. The operational scenario is being finalized with the user representative. The development of a template for the analyzer has begun.	12 months	12 months
Vulnerability analyzer[c]	The template is working according to the operational scenario. The first instance of the analyzer will be available in the next iteration.	9 months	9 months
Security Services			
Consulting	Staff with security expertise have been hired and are available. They have full knowledge of the tools and services to be offered.	9 months	Available now
Penetration testing	The operational scenario is being finalized.	12 months	12 months
Security assessment	The process of defining the operational scenario has begun.	15 months	15 months
Security training and mentoring	The curricula has been defined, and so have the courses in design and development. We must delay delivery because we're using real examples from practice in training.	Phased starting in 9 months	12 months
Vulnerability analysis	The operational scenario has been defined, and automation is almost complete.	9 months	9 months

[a] Dashboard needed in initial delivery to invoke tools and coordinate their activities

[b] Will license scanner from commercial vendor instead of developing it

[c] Tool needed to run vulnerability analyses

TABLE 7-5 Key wins associated with the use of Agile methods.

Agile Practice Adopted	Key Win
Capture requirements via user stories	Features and content have driven development rather than specifications.
Form self-organizing teams	Focus has been on team throughput rather than on individual productivity.
Plan iteratively at the beginning of each iteration	Work has been prioritized for the team and its members. Releases have been time-boxed and predictable.
Deliver frequently (daily builds preferred)	A working product has been visible within weeks of the start, not months. Potential releases have been every six weeks, not every year.
Plan to learn—welcome changing requirements throughout the project	There has been flexibility to address changing user requirements throughout the development cycle.
Emphasize simplicity in architecture and design	Team has kept things simple and reduced potential volatility.
Test everything	There has been a continuous focus on testing from start to finish.
Communicate powerfully in daily stand-up meetings	Everyone knows what is going on and what is expected of them.
Measure value—working software is the primary measure of progress	Daily metric drumbeats were established that provided insight into the health and status of the product.

Outcomes and lessons learned

Confidence in you and your team was restored at the meeting. You did this by answering most of the questions related to the status prior to the event. That does not mean there was not any criticism and redirection provided by management. That would be unthinkable because that is their job. However, you were surprised when quality assurance slammed you at the meeting for not capturing defect information. They argued that you needed to make sure quality was up to standards by analyzing defect data. Because quality was the discriminator in the marketplace, delivering poor quality to meet the schedule would lead to catastrophe. Based on these inputs at the meeting, you took the following four actions:

- To acquire needed security knowledge, your firm purchased a small business specializing in security analysis and vulnerability training. You then moved several key people from this firm to all of your locations and put them to work mentoring your teams. Moving people was not an issue because the firm your company purchased was from Idaho and many of the people there wanted either to get away from the long winters or to get closer to their families.

- To speed up the delivery of your training services, you tasked personnel from the training firm to develop the security courseware using examples taken from the test team's efforts to qualify the software. Then you instructed these security experts to replace these examples with examples taken from the practice later, when there is time. This action should enable you to offer training and mentoring upon product release, not three months later.

- To reduce management's and marketing's concerns, you provide them with bi-weekly progress reports and hold a monthly status review. In the reports, you provide the velocity status for each iteration and the shippable increment by team and product offering.

- You capture software defect metrics and report them monthly to provide evidence that the quality of products being shipped to the field is up to par and will not taint the reputation of the company. You employ the data in a software-defect removal model[9] and use it to make decisions about when and when not to ship the product.

The lessons learned in this Agile methods project were many and include, but are not limited to, the following:

- Be advised that risk increases dramatically when embracing new methods to bring new products to market according to an aggressive schedule.

- When embracing new methods such as Agile, do not lose sight of the marketplace discriminators (such as quality, in our case study). Make sure that you measure whether you have accounted for these discriminators, because they are as important as, or more important than, throughput and other delivery measures.

- It is important to recognize the power of problem-domain knowledge. Without this specific knowledge, it is very difficult to build products that will be suited for the marketplace.

- What works in the small does not always work as well in the large. This cautions us to be extremely careful when we try to apply lessons learned in the small because they do not always work within a larger context when they are engaged.

- Although Agile methods apparently provide added value, the issues involved in adopting and scaling them are immense. If you do not have the time to deal with all the relevant issues, bring in professionals to help you figure out how to best use these methods. You will be glad that you did once the dust settles.

- Providing just-in-time training is advantageous because it develops skills, knowledge, and abilities when you need them.

- When adopting new methods such as Agile, look as carefully at the user of the method as at the method. Not all users are mature enough to handle new concepts like these. However, in many cases, they can overcome their handicaps when you embrace change-management principles and deploy them in a highly structured and logical manner.

- Do not forget the importance of communications, including keeping your company's management apprised of your progress and project issues. If you don't give them current information, their support can waiver seemingly overnight, even when you have high-level champions for change in your corner. Having cascading sponsorship at levels below the executive sponsor is also another key to success.

- When scaling Agile projects, some compromises have to be made. The goal is to reach the balance between agility and discipline[10] that is needed to maintain your pace and achieve stability.

- The best way to quiet your critics is to deliver results. The ability to deliver what you promise is what counts in most firms.

Summary

This chapter discussed how easy it is to loosen discipline and lose sight of one of your primary goals as you get caught up with developing a technology. In this case, Agile methods were used to advantage as a firm hurried to market with a new software product line. The new technology was exciting, and a lot of effort was expended as Agile methods were systematically exploited to get the products out of the door. As the methods were introduced, the discipline associated with keeping management apprised of progress and change-management principles—particularly those involving ongoing communications with management, marketing, and quality assurance—were forgotten. More importantly, the company's focus on quality, which served as the marketplace discriminator in this case, was lost momentarily. The organizational focus placed on quality saved the day, as did the decision to purchase a firm that provided problem-domain knowledge. However, without the focus on quality and the problem that needed to be solved, the reminders that were provided to embrace quality would have been disregarded as Agile methods were introduced.

References

References cited within this chapter include the following:

[1] See the following site for information on the Agile Manifesto: *http://agilemanifesto.org*.

[2] Erik Moore and John Spens, "Scaling Agile: Finding Your Agile Tribe," *Proceedings of the Agile 2008 Conference*, IEEE Computer Society, August 2008, pp. 121-124.

[3] Mike Cohn, *User Stories Applied: For Agile Software Development* (Addison-Wesley, 2004).

[4] Martin Fowler, Kent Beck, John Brant, William Opdike, and Don Roberts, *Refactoring: Improving the Design of Existing Code* (Addison-Wesley, 1999).

[5] Laurie Williams and Robert Kessler, *Pair Programming Illuminated* (Addison-Wesley, 2002).

[6] Kent Beck, *Test Driven Development: An Example* (Addison-Wesley, 2002).

[7] A good explanation of velocity can be found at the following site: *http://www.versionone.com/Agile101/velocity.asp*.

[8] Richard H. Franke and James D. Kaul, "The Hawthorne Experiments: First Statistical Interpretations," *American Sociological Review*, 1978, pp. 623-643.

[9] Sunita Chulani and Barry Boehm, *Modeling Software Defect Introduction and Removal*, University of Southern California, Report No. USC-CSE-99-520, 1999.

[10] Barry Boehm and Richard Turner, *Balancing Agility and Discipline: A Guide for the Perplexed* (Addison-Wesley, 2003).

Web resources

Applicable web resources that amplify points made in this chapter can be found here:

- Amazon has many books and articles on Agile methods. Go to *www.amazon.com* and search under *agile methods* to find relevant citations.

- The Agile Alliance is an international industry group established to foster the use of Agile methods. It does this by putting on conferences, workshops, and training events. It also provides a free article library, videos, and presentations, and it publishes a newsletter and surveys. The Alliance site is located at *http://www.agilealliance.org*.

- Many Agile vendors offer lots of resources on their websites. For example, Rally Software provides free white papers, presentations, webinars, and articles at the following site: *http://www.rallydev.com/downloads*. VersionOne is a second vendor that provides links to many useful Agile sites, at *http://www.versionone.com/Agile101/Community.asp*.

- Many advocates for Agile methods also offer case studies. Two of the better ones I have read are at *http://www.thoughtworks-studios.com/resources/case-studies* and *http://citeseerx.ist.psu.edu/viewdoc/download?doi=10.1.1.87.6278&rep=rep1&type=pdf*.

- An interesting and still valid assessment of Agile technology written in 2005 is available from Nokia at *http://www.agile-itea.org/public/deliverables/ITEA-AGILE-D5.2.3_v1.0.pdf*.

- Besides providing Agile resources from its library, the Data & Analysis Center for Software maintains a current list of Agile discussion groups, list servers, and blogs at *http://www.thedacs.com/databases/url/key/3990/4945*.

- There are lots of training firms that offer hands-on training in the various Agile methods. You might consider visiting one of the following sites for popular course offerings: *http://www.objectmentor.com/omSolutions/agile_training.html*, *http://agiletraining.com/#*, and *http://www.aspe-sdlc.com/agiletraining.php?gclid=COmfmbi00aoCFQ6AgwodzX7Qzw*.

- For those of you in the defense business thinking that the Department of Defense (DOD) does not use Agile, let me refer you to a recent handbook by MITRE Corporation titled "Handbook for Implementing Agile in Department of Defense Information Technology Acquisition" at *http://www.mitre.org/work/tech_papers/2011/11_0401/11_0401.pdf*.

- For those interested in cyber threats, MITRE maintains a number of sites for Department of Homeland Security (DHS) and DOD that highlight vulnerabilities and software weaknesses. See the Common Vulnerabilities and Exposures (CVE) and Common Weaknesses Enumeration (CWE) sites at *http://cve.mitre.org* and *http://cwe.mitre.org* for more details.

CHAPTER 8

Government Case:
Large Defense Project Behind
Schedule and Over Budget

Setting the stage

Your firm received a large contract award six months ago from the Department of Defense (DOD) to develop the next-generation workstation for use in the command-and-control families of unmanned aerial vehicles (UAVs) across the armed services. This is a software-intensive effort aimed at building the best-of-breed workstation that all UAV projects in the DOD will migrate to over the next decade. Commercial off-the-shelf (COTS) hardware, the POSIX operating system, and the Apache platform will be used as the foundation of the service-oriented architecture you have proposed to implement. Your firm is thrilled to have won this project, which it estimates can generate several billion dollars in revenue if successful.

The competition for the contract was fierce, and your firm had to be very aggressive to win the competition. The team promised a lot as they cut costs to the bone. The two other bidders protested the award, and there was a delay of almost eight months as you waited for the protest to be resolved. The net result was that almost all the key staff named in the proposal that the project was counting on had to be assigned to other jobs. In addition, the contract that was awarded was incrementally funded, which resulted in your team receiving funds to do only part of the job. Your job is to lead the effort once the contract is awarded. In addition, the colonel who the DOD put in charge of managing the contractual effort has stated that, this time, the DOD will do the job right. What that means, nobody seems to know. However, everyone on the team has a bad feeling every time they hear him utter this statement.

Organization

The project has been organized as illustrated in Figure 8-1 to comply with the DOD's desire for emphasis on both project management and product line management. The project team reports directly to the vice president in charge of Defense programs. The customer organization you will interface with is shown at the bottom of this figure.

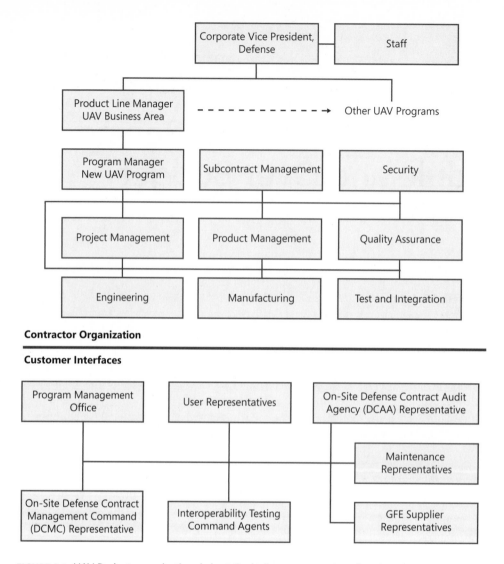

Contractor Organization

Customer Interfaces

FIGURE 8-1 UAV Project organizational chart (including customer interfaces).

The effort will be parceled out according to the teaming agreement shown in Table 8-1 to provide the skills needed to get the job done as scoped in the draft Concept of Operations (CONOPS), System Specification, and software specifications. These documents were submitted along with your proposal to give those making the selection decision insight into how you would approach the job if you were awarded the contract.

TABLE 8-1 Primary teammates and their roles and skills.

Teammates	Roles	Skills
Your Division Los Angeles, CA	Integration and Overall Program Management	System development, integration, and management of delivery.
Sister Division Dallas, TX	Aerial Vehicle	Airborne platform development, and its life-cycle support.
Sister Division Arlington, VA	Ground Station	Command-and-control platform development, and its life-cycle support.
Subcontractor Chicago, IL	Communications	Communications equipment production, and its life-cycle support.
Subcontractor Indianapolis, IN	Diagnostics and Self-Healing Technologies	Diagnostic and self-healing equipment concepts, and its life-cycle support.
Subcontractor Macon, GA	Specialized Interfaces and Interoperability Testing and Analysis	Interfaces across military networks, and associated interoperability testing and analysis.
Subcontractor Iselin, NJ	Independent Verification and Validation (IV&V)	Small business that can provide IV&V support for the Program Office.
Subcontractor Dayton, OH	Safety Analysis and Certification	Small business that specializes in safety analysis and certifications.
Many hardware vendors (all based in offices in the United States)	Platform	Vendors selected to provide COTS hardware platforms, including gateways and networking equipment. Specialized firewalls, intrusion detection, and other devices to protect the network are also included in the mix.
Many software suppliers (based in offices in the United States and Puerto Rico)	Platform	Vendors selected to provide systems software (operating systems, utilities, and so forth), applications, and tools under license that run on the selected platforms. Specialized computer performance evaluation software is included in the mix, as is wideband communications between sites.

As shown in Figure 8-1, the customer plans to provide many resources to help you get your job done. These include on-site contract and management representatives who they expect you to invite to your internal team meetings. They have also identified the following nine working groups and Integrated Product Teams (IPTs)[1] that they want you to staff during the effort:

- Aerial Vehicle IPT

- Configuration Control Working Group

- Ground Station IPT

- Interface Control Working Group

- Interoperability Test Working Group

- Metrics Working Group

- Risk Management Working Group

- Transition and Turnover Working Group

- Integration Working Group

As noted in Table 8-1, two sister groups within your firm that have different skill sets will work with your division to get the job done. The reason for this according to the grapevine is that all three groups need the work to avoid potential layoffs because of cutbacks in other areas.

In addition to these organizational interfaces, numerous other subcontracts and a large number of COTS hardware and software vendors are involved in the effort. Licenses will be an issue, as will purchase agreements. There are also government inputs in the form of interface specification and specialized software to test the externally developed software packages that have been promised to you as either Government Furnished Information (GFI) or Government Furnished Equipment (GFE).

Project

You are in charge of the software effort. As with many large defense contracts of this nature, software represents the majority of the engineering work and risk on the contract. But there is not a single person above the rank of task leader in either the firm's or customer's organizations with a software background. The firm's management has hardware experience and training, while the customer's leads have acquisition, finance, and/or operational backgrounds.

The goal of the project is to deliver the next-generation UAV system within three years for a cost not to exceed $750 million. This next-generation UAV system will be able to autonomously seek out and destroy targets based on a predetermined mission plan with a 90 percent success rate. Should components fail on-board the aerial vehicle, the system should be able to heal itself and return to base.

Process

The software development effort is scoped to deliver the subsystems identified in Table 8-2. As shown in the table, these software subsystems will be supplied iteratively[2] over three years in three builds as hardware is delivered. The purpose of developing the software in this manner is to demonstrate progress as risk is managed and requirements are pinned down.

Requirements volatility is high for two reasons. First, the customer user representatives are arguing over the controls and displays. One wants you to build 3D displays, while the other wants virtual reality displays. Because neither option was proposed, both introduce an element of uncertainty into the design. Second, the customer maintenance representatives are making life unbearable. They want the new system to be fully upward compatible with the one it is replacing, which was built in the late 1980s. Going backwards in time is not what your design team contemplated when drafting the CONOPS and requirements that were delivered with the proposal. It represents a major design change that seems unacceptable to everyone but the maintenance team.

TABLE 8-2 Software products and deliverables.

Subsystem	Software Product	Build 1	Build 2	Build 3
Aerial System	Guidance, Navigation, and Control (GNC)	X		
	Command and Data Subsystem	X		
	Autonomous Mission Management Subsystem		X	
	Diagnosis and Self-Healing Subsystem			X
Ground System	Displays and Controls	X		
	Mission Planning, Management, and Command Subsystem	X		
	Weapons Management Subsystem		X	
	Simulation and Training System		X	
	Diagnosis Subsystem			X
Communications System	Network Management Subsystem	X		
	Wideband Communications		X	
	Protection Subsystem			X
Platform	System Software (Ground)	X		
	System Software (Aerial Vehicle)	X		
Software Development and Management Facilities	Software Environment (including toolset)	X		
	UAV Project Web Portal		X	
	Performance Evaluation Subsystem			X

Note that the firm made a significant investment in the process in anticipation of the contract. It updated its process and got reappraised at CMMI[3] Level 4 via a Standard CMMI Appraisal Method for Process Improvement (SCAMPI)[4] one year prior to the solicitation being delivered. Your firm also required that each of its software subcontractors be currently appraised at least at CMMI Level 3. Several have already received higher ratings. As part of the proposal activity, the firm formed working groups to address the use of common processes and tools for such core software activities as configuration management, distribution control, documentation, metrics, and project-management tracking. For software development, it was agreed that your organization would develop a common software development environment for the project that each of the subcontractors would interface their own toolsets to in order to house the build and deliverable baselines in a centralized repository. Finally, everyone on the team thought that the development and use of a common web portal for communications and for sharing the work in process was a great idea.

Product

The products you will build, their size, and the budgets allocated are summarized in Table 8-3. Budgets were allocated after fierce battles with management over justification. They just did not understand why software seemed to cost so much. They argued that according to the movie *The Social Network*, college kids allegedly generate thousands of lines of code overnight. "Why, then, is the productivity of the software engineering shop so low in comparison," they want to know. Luckily, the product line manager for the UAV Business Area has been through the arguments before and came to the software division's defense. He also helped you push through reasonable budgets for support tasks (product management and other such tasks) and project-management activities. However, even then, you still had to take a large budget cut because management just could not see any justification for the larger allocations you requested. Software, rightfully or wrongly, received 32 percent of the total budget allocated to the project, which was $750 million. The cuts were put into the program reserve supposedly to address risks and problems that might arise during the project.

TABLE 8-3 Size and budget by subsystem and software product.

Subsystem	Software Product	Size (in SLOC)[a]	Budget
Aerial System	Guidance, Navigation, and Control (GNC) Command and Data Subsystem Autonomous Mission Management Subsystem Diagnosis and Self-Healing Subsystem	100,000 200,000 200,000 100,000	$15,000,000 $30,000,000 $25,000,000 $10,000,000
Ground System	Displays and Controls Mission Planning, Management, and Command Subsystem Weapons Management Subsystem Simulation and Training System Diagnosis Subsystem	200,000 700,000 Government provided 300,000 100,000	$5,000,000 $70,000,000 $1,000,000 $15,000,000 $4,000,000
Communications System	Network Management Subsystem Wideband Communications Protection Subsystem	COTS COTS COTS	$250,000 $100,000 $250,000
Platform	System Software (Ground) System Software (Aerial Vehicle)	COTS COTS	$150,000 $250,000
Software Development and Management Facilities	Software Environment (including toolset) Software Management Web System Performance Evaluation Subsystem	COTS COTS COTS	$350,000 $50,000 $100,000
Software Integration	Integration and Test Support to Systems IPTs	TOTAL	$28,000,000
Software Project Management	Project Management Supplier Management	TOTAL	$23,000,000
Software Product Management	Configuration Management Quality Assurance IV&V Safety Engineering Reliability Engineering Metrics	TOTAL	$12,500,000
TOTALS		**1,900,000**	**$240,000,000**

[a] Source lines of code

People

The skill, knowledge, and ability requirements for the workforce needed to deliver this system within three years are exceptionally high. That is the reason you have so many subcontractors on the team. You wanted to be able to start the software development effort the moment the contract was awarded. You did three other things to help with the staffing. First, you secured a promise from your vice president that he would provide you with sufficient funds so that every software-related person in your organization would have a minimum of one week of paid training a year for the full term of the contract. Next, you brought a small firm onboard to hire contract labor. Unlike most body shops, this firm primarily hires people in the area who have retired from DOD jobs and have the right background and skills to help on the project. As your staff needs vary based on workload, you will use them to cover the peaks and valleys. As your third action, you put 25 of your most promising software technical personnel through a six-week, intensive, hands-on training program in software project management. The program offers those who complete the course a certificate in project management. Because the certificate is prestigious within the firm, holders are placed on the fast-track promotion cycle. These graduates will also assume primary leadership roles for the development effort. In addition, several of the more promising graduates will be selected to assume major management roles at subcontractor plants.

With regard to your software subcontractors, you made it a requirement in their contract that you will have approval rights for replacement of any of their key personnel. You also had them provide a skills inventory so that you can tap them for talent should the need arise. You also established a software working group in which key software personnel on the project meet or hold teleconferences to discuss technical and management issues they view as important. The teleconferences take place on a twice-weekly basis, on Tuesday and Friday afternoons at 3 p.m. These are working sessions in which your bosses are definitely not invited to attend, even though they want to.

With regard to COTS vendors, you view several of them as so important that you dedicated people to be relationship managers with them. You also had the vendors agree to provide personnel who will be on-site to add insight and support during the development should problems arise.

As noted in Table 8-1, the team is dispersed geographically throughout the United States and Puerto Rico. The firm has already taken actions to address potential geographical distance problems. It installed wideband communications, including secure links between key players. It has dedicated space in two buildings to co-locate the team members, which includes supplier representatives and members of the IV&V team. The firm is also developing a dedicated web portal for this UAV project on which it will host information of interest for the team, specifications, and other documentation and work in progress. The portal will be part of the software environment that is being put together to provide a common toolset and management infrastructure for software development. When the environment is operational in about three months, teammates will be required to link their internal production-control systems to this portal and make their products available to those who need them to perform their jobs, using strict access-control guidelines. Finally, your firm has placed management teams at all of your major subcontractor plants to provide oversight and direction on a day-to-day basis. When you query your customer representatives about these actions, they tell you they viewed these arrangements as one of the major strengths of your proposal.

Options, recommendations, and reactions

Because of the delays in awarding the contract and the forecast that the software team will peak at 450 professionals by the end the year, staffing the team has been, and continues to be, a problem. It seems that none of the organizations involved with the software development effort can staff the project quickly enough to gain momentum and start satisfying the schedule. The management indicators that are being used to assess progress show that you are already three months behind, six months into the effort. Obviously, both your management and the customer are concerned. They conduct a review to determine the root causes of the problem and what to do about them. They listen and react by saying that instead of excuses they want to hear what you are doing to solve the problem. You have one week to get back to them with a set of recommendations.

You start your fact-finding effort by looking at the staffing actual results versus the plans. As illustrated in Figure 8-2, the major shortfalls in staff can be localized to two sites: your sister division building at the ground station in Arlington, VA, and the diagnosis and self-healing technologies subcontractor in Indianapolis, IN. Both are experiencing startup problems. Your team in Arlington reports that getting staff is proving harder than anticipated because your sister organization just won another big defense contract and they are having difficulty staffing both contracts at the same time. This is a major concern that needs to be resolved quickly because parts of the ground station are on the critical path for the first build. Because the effort is much smaller and the product is not needed until the third build, the diagnosis and self-healing technologies subcontractor's problem seems less critical. They still require immediate attention, but you feel that you have time available to correct the situation. You also notice that your own staffing performance is not up to par.

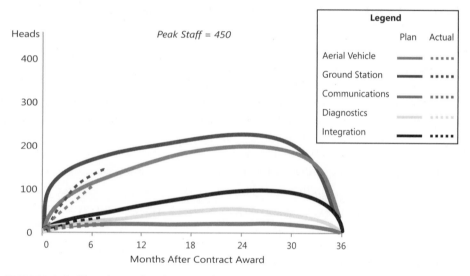

FIGURE 8-2 Staffing plans and performance (first six months).

Based on the information you have gathered, you now proceed to work with your staff to develop the options for the three organizations that seem to be at the root cause of the staff problem. These are summarized in Table 8-4. Your recommended actions are identified by the shaded boxes in the table. As an additional action, senior management needs to pressure your sister organization and get it to perform to satisfy its commitments.

TABLE 8-4 Options and recommended actions for addressing staffing issues.

Organization	Issue	Option	Impact
Ground Station Arlington, VA	There are two big contracts and not enough people to work on both.	Hire more people.	May have to orient and train; may make late project later (Brooks Law).[5]
		Hire contractors.	Offload near-term work to skilled contract labor until employees become available.
		Move the job elsewhere.	Sister groups do not have the skills.
Diagnosis and Self-Healing Technologies Indianapolis, IN	People are busy on other jobs that are running late.	Speed up the transition.	Put pressure on subcontractor to speed up the transition and get the job done.
		Hire more people.	This is a budget buster.
Your Division Los Angeles, CA	People are responding to fires and not able to get to work.	Buffer your workers, and put them to work.	Use line management to handle fires as best they can, thereby freeing up people to do integration planning.
		Hire more people.	This is a budget buster.

Outcomes and lessons learned

At the end of the week, you feel prepared. The meeting with management is scheduled for 10 a.m. in the large conference room. When you show up, you are amazed. The room, which has a capacity of 50, already has 80 people in it—with more arriving every minute. The program manager makes a command decision to move the meeting to the auditorium. When the dust settles down, there are over 100 people in the room. More than half of the attendees are government people, many of whom flew in because they were advised you were in trouble.

The meeting starts out with the VP taking the stage and welcoming everyone to the facility. Next, the government program manager gets up and says a few words that emphasize the importance of the job. Your boss, the head of engineering, then gets up and sets the stage by joking about how software is always in trouble. It is now your turn to talk. You briefly outline the issues as you see them, present the data you collected, and make your recommendations. Of course, you field lots of questions. But most of them are easy because they are from people who want to be seen and heard by the big shots and who know little about the subject area. You feel pretty good at the end of your pitch.

After a short break, your company's management team discusses the recommendations. Of course, they are less than candid with so many customer representatives in the room demanding action. They agree to adopt your recommendations and generate reports highlighting how well they are working on a weekly basis. These reports will be delivered via e-mail to the customer to highlight your progress. However, the customer does not seem satisfied. They want to increase their on-site presence to monitor the situation and gather data in a more hands-on way. They seem very distrustful and want their own people to keep them informed of the progress. With so many people in the room, your bosses have only one option. They agree with the customer's demands and take the action to find office space for the government's team to take up residence.

At the end of the meeting, one of the subject matter experts from one of the government think-tanks takes the stage to comment on the situation. He defends you, saying that you have done many positive things to reduce risk and that the government is being overly critical. He goes on to make the following additional recommendations, which seem to fall on deaf ears:

- Elevate software organizationally and have the software manager report directly to the program manager instead of to the engineering director.

- Simplify accountability by clarifying responsibility and lines of communications.

- Develop cost-to-complete and schedule-to-complete estimates from this date forward.

- Based on the new plan, reallocate resources and restart the effort with a clean slate.

The lessons learned in this large defense project were many and include, but are not limited to, the following:

- Applying change-management principles—particularly those involving communications with key stakeholders, including customers and senior management—is a critical success factor.

- It is a rare occasion when upper management understands software. What I have observed is that most senior managers from outside of the software business come from non-technical disciplines like finance, marketing, and/or the law. The reason for this is simple. They are elevated to senior positions because they have the skills needed to address the major issues their firm is facing today and into the future.

- Few senior managers really understand what it takes to design, develop, and field a world-class software product. They just do not fathom the resources required.

- Even a well-planned and executed software program can get into trouble, especially when external events conspire to cause the problem (such as the sister division winning another large job and causing conflicts for resources, as in this case).

- When addressing an issue, look for the root cause. Most people treat the symptoms because they do not dig deeply enough to find the real reasons they are having problems.

- When looking for the root cause, investigate your actual performance data and look at the indicators. What they tell you is normally right, especially when you trust their integrity.

- Talk to the people involved in the decisions about the issues to understand their thoughts and viewpoints. Often those close to a problem understand it and have very useful ideas on how to address it.

- Simple solutions to difficult problems often do not work well. For example, hiring untrained staff to cope with a staffing-up problem can often cause the project to be further delayed.

- The customer is always right, no matter what. If the customer wants to send in a team to monitor issues, let them. But recognize that their need might be driven by other factors. In our case, the customer did not trust the contractor to provide them with the facts.

- Watch out—if you are not careful, your customer might provide you help that is unwanted. Often, such assistance is more damaging than helpful.

Summary

This chapter provides insights into large defense contracts and how they are organized, staffed, and managed. The major issues that occur during execution all tend to stem from size. Just keeping a workforce of 450 software professionals pointed in the same direction when they are geographically dispersed and working for different firms is a challenge. Then add the difficulties that can arise due to complicated interfaces, demanding customers, and a distrustful environment and it is no wonder that the success rates reported for large defense projects are so low.[6] I will have much more to say on this topic in later Department of Defense case studies, where we investigate how to increase this success rate as we cope with other issues that arise.

References

References cited within this chapter include the following:

[1] Steve Mills, "We Don't Dance Well," *Defense AT&L,* March-April 2010, accessible at: *http:/www.dau.mil/pubscats/ATL%20Docs/Mar-Apr10/mills_mar-apr10.pdf*

[2] Craig Larman, *Agile and Iterative Development: A Manager's Guide* (Addison-Wesley, 2003).

[3] Mary Beth Chrisis, Mike Konrad, and Sandra Shrum, *CMMI for Development: Guidelines for Process Integration and Product Improvement,* 3rd ed. (Addison-Wesley, 2011).

[4] Dennis M. Ahern, Jim Armstrong, Aaron Clouse, and Jack R. Ferguson, *CMMI SCAMPI Distilled: Appraisals for Process Improvement* (Addison-Wesley, 2005).

[5] Frederick P. Brooks, *The Mythical Man-Month: Essays on Software Engineering,* 2nd ed. (Addison-Wesley, 1995).

[6] U.S. Government Accountability Office (GAO), *Defense Acquisitions: Assessment of Selected Weapons Programs,* Report GAO-08-467SP, March 2008.

Web resources

Applicable web resources that amplify points made in this chapter can be found here:

- One of my favorite sites for materials on project management is the Project Management Institute at *http://www.pmi.org*. Besides publishing the Project Management Body of Knowledge (PMBOK), this organization publishes interesting articles, runs seminars, and holds conferences on project-management topics.

- Another useful site belongs to Defense Acquisition University at *http://www.dau.mil*. Besides running university and certificate courses, this organization publishes journals and has a library of publications on software-acquisition-management topics.

- The Deputy Director for Acquisition Management's site at the Department of Defense provides useful pointers to information (earned value and other topics) to those interested in such topics at the following site: *http://www.acq.osd.mil/ara/office-am.htm*.

- The following site provides links to about 100 other sites providing project, program, and acquisition-management information: *http://www.niwotridge.com/Resources/PM-SWEResources/PMSites.htm*.

- Many federal acquisition groups provide resources for those interested in receiving contracts from them. For example, the Forest Service site can be found at the following link: *http://www.fs.fed.us/business/incident/vendorsupport.php*.

- In addition to offering degree programs, many service schools such as the Naval Postgraduate School (NPS) offer reports, theses, and dissertations on relevant topics. As an example, NPS reports of potential interest can be found by searching the following site: *http://www.nps.edu/research/TechReports.html*.

- The Defense Acquisition Portal supported by the Defense Acquisition University provides a one-stop source for acquisition-management information and tools at *https://dap.dau.mil*.

CHAPTER 9

Government Case: Introducing New Technology

Setting the stage

You have been working on a government research and development (R&D) contract to develop and mature a new technology for protecting network-based systems against attacks from intruders, both insiders and hackers, for the past six years. The defenses you invented (and which you have patent applications for) are called *active defenses*.

The defenses work by first identifying the attack scenario. Attacks are represented next in the form of a state vector, which is designed to capture and communicate as much information about the attack as possible. As the attack unfolds, these state vectors are updated with the dynamics of the attack. The defenses take the information and use game theory algorithms that exploit the Nash equilibrium concept[1] to determine how best to defeat the intruder. The worst case solution is a draw, which means the intruder goes in circles but does not get into the network. Interim solutions are represented in the form of another set of state vectors that contain constraints and transition information. The algorithms reconfigure the defenses as a function of time to ward off the attack as more knowledge about the attack is communicated via the state vectors. There is no need to hide information because the algorithms assume that the intruder has full knowledge of your defenses.

During the first two years of the effort, you developed the algorithms and validated them through a series of experiments. There was a lot of tweaking as the algorithms' parameters and optimality criteria were changed so that they could home in on an equilibrium solution. Because the Nash algorithms are extremely complex, learning how to manipulate them took some time and mathematical talent. When they were mastered in the second year of the effort, they were extended and adapted so that they could be used for this new purpose. The key innovation was the use of state vectors to capture and communicate knowledge about the dynamics.

During the next two years, tools were developed to make use of the algorithms easier. This toolset was then used to defend a simulated network against an organized attack to validate the algorithm's potential. Results were also compared line by line against a hand-calculated solution to ensure bit-for-bit fidelity with the mathematical algorithms. Because this activity went well, the customer funded the follow-on activity, which was directed toward using the algorithms on a pilot project that allowed testing under representative operational conditions.

Finding a pilot defense project for the next two years of the effort turned out to be quite a challenge. Even with the sponsor's active support, all of the people involved with defense projects who you spoke with declined your offer to collaborate because they were afraid of the potential negative impacts associated with the use of what they considered a new and risky technology. The few project personnel who expressed interest refused to pilot the technology after some internal debate because of what they called "operational security issues." This really meant that they just could not secure permission to use the active-defense technology on an active network.

A commercial firm came in and saved the day. You met their chief engineer at a security conference, where he was looking for innovations in network security. This firm is in the gambling business in Nevada. They are one of the largest slot machine manufacturers in the business. They also operate machines that are placed in remote locations such as airports, gas stations, grocery stores, malls, and a host of other frequently visited places. When placed into operation, the machines are networked together and monitored at a central site because security in remote areas has been an issue. The machines also are programmed to send reports every hour to the central site on gambling activity and winnings. Such reports are constantly analyzed for suspicious activity using very sophisticated algorithms, and armed security teams are dispatched if there are signs of trouble. Management of the firm is interested in the active-defense technology because they had been repeatedly attacked by gangs of criminals who were using handheld devices to gain access and change the odds so that gang members playing the machines would win big jackpots. No two machines were ever targeted in the same area, and the players were in disguises. The agreement reached after lots of discussion and negotiation between this gambling firm, you, and your government sponsor was that all experiments on the network would be on a noninterference basis. In addition, visits to facilities would be controlled and publications would have to be approved by both the government and the gambling firm.

The past two years were spent working with the commercial firm to perfect the algorithms, enhance the toolset, and create an active-defense demonstration test bed to show off the potential of the technology to prospective users of this defense technology. This effort was very rewarding because it showed that the technology indeed held a lot of promise. It also demonstrated the merits of using Agile methods[2] to develop the toolset. Obviously, the gambling firm you were working with is interested in the technology and willing to buy the sole rights to retain it as its intellectual property. But agreements you have with the government prohibit you from doing this. The best you can offer the gambling firm is an exclusive five-year license to use the technology and associated toolset within the commercial gaming business area. To get this agreement, you spent a lot of time with government attorneys, whose position was that the government paid to develop the technology and therefore retains ownership rights for it. However, they are willing to give up the commercial rights in the future for some consideration if the technology pans out and is used extensively by military projects.

You are currently working on the final two years of the effort. This activity is directed toward what the government calls *commercialization of technology.* During this period, you try to stimulate widespread use of the technology in Department of Defense (DOD) projects. You are tasked with developing a commercialization plan. You have some core funds to make a product with the technology. A "product" in this sense is the technology packaged for consumption by target users with white papers, manuals, training, customer support, and other such items. There is even money available for the first company that comes forward and says it will use the technology that will be provided on a cost-sharing basis with a 50:50 split. In other words, your sponsor will match the project's expenditures dollar for dollar if that company commits funds for your commercialization effort. Because of your past failures when trying to get projects committed as pilots, you have asked your government sponsor for help in preparing a plan, the outline of which is summarized in Figure 9-1.

"Wow," you think when you look at what has to be done. "Do I really have to do all of this to commercialize a technology?" It should be noted that a National Science Foundation (NSF) outline[3] was used by the customer for the plan because it took a more commercial flavor.

Organization

Looking at the commercialization plan outline, you realize that you have to reorganize. Your firm is a small business that specializes in software development and R&D for defense contracts. You employ just over 200 professionals using the organizational structure shown in Figure 9-2. You modify this structure to add dedicated resources for marketing and outreach. You also create an advisory board to help you understand and tailor your active-defense technology for defense project needs. Of course, the chief engineer from the gambling firm will also be a member of this board because you want to satisfy commercial needs as well. The major change to your organization is the addition of a customer service group. Members of this team will staff the help desk and generate needed product support materials. Funding for these organizational changes comes from profits because the advisory board and customer support group will service clients at large, not a specific client. However, funding for products generated by this group for commercializing the active-defense technology will at least partially come from the contract with the government because this is in line with its scope.

1. Market Opportunity
a. Describe succinctly what product or service you are planning to deliver based on your innovation.
b. What customer needs will be addressed with your product or service?
c. Describe who your target customer is—providing generally known examples may be helpful.
d. How does the target customer currently meet the need you are addressing? Or convincingly describe how there is a significant problem that is not yet being addressed.
e. What is the business model you plan to adopt to generate revenue from your innovation?
f. How do you plan to exit the investment?
g. Is the target market domestic, international, or both?
h. Describe the channels you would employ to reach the targeted customer.
i. What is the current size of the broad market you plan to enter and the niche market opportunity you are addressing?
j. What are the growth trends for the market and the key trends in the industry that you are planning to target?
k. What are the barriers to entering this market?
l. Describe the technology/development objectives and critical milestones that must be met to address the market opportunity.
m. If there are potential societal, educational, or scientific benefits beyond commercial considerations, they should be included here and explained in sufficient detail to convey the significance of the effort.

2. Company/Team
a. Provide a short description of the origins of the company.
b. What type of corporate structure is in place?
c. What is the current capitalization?
d. What is the current employee count?
e. What is the revenue history for the past three years?
f. What are the sources of operating capital or revenue: product sales, consulting/services, license revenues, R&D grants/contracts, and other sources?
g. Give a brief description of the experience and credentials of the personnel responsible for taking the innovation to market.
h. What specific experience does the team lack, and how will this be addressed during the Phase II effort and beyond?
i. How does the background and experience of the team enhance the credibility of the commercialization plan? Have they previously taken similar products/services to market?
j. From what additional resources do you have commitment (Board of Directors, Board of Advisors, Technical Advisors, Legal Counsel, etc.)? Provide details on the names, affiliations, and expertise of these resources.

3. Product/Technology and Competition
a. What are the critical needs ("pain points") that your product or service is fulfilling for your customer?
b. What features of your technology will allow you to provide a compelling value proposition? How have you validated the significance of these features?
c. What is your customer willing to pay for your product or service? How have you validated this assumption?
d. What are your costs to produce the product or service? What are the assumptions that underlie your cost model(s)?
e. How does your technology/innovation allow your team to compete and win in the marketplace?
f. How does your product or service match up to that of the competition?
g. What do you anticipate the competitive landscape to look like when you get to market?
h. Describe the intellectual property landscape.
i. Do you have the freedom to operate?
j. How do you plan to protect the intellectual property associated with your technology?
k. What other sources of intellectual property will you need to access in order to address the market opportunity described above?

4. Finance and Revenue Model
a. Describe an appropriate staged finance plan given the market opportunity described above; enumerate the level of funding required for each stage along the path to commercialization.
b. How will you access the appropriate funds? Provide specific contacts, leads, previous relationships, and agreements already in place.
c. What commitments do you have for follow-on funding?
d. Describe the revenue streams (licensing, product sales, or other) associated with your commercialization plan. What are the adoption rates?
e. When do you anticipate first revenues from each stream?
f. When do you expect to reach breakeven?
g. Provide annual pro forma financial statements for the next five years (2 years of the Phase II effort plus 3 years of the post–Phase II effort). Income statements are required. Cash flow information and balance sheets can be included if they are considered critical for your strategy. If not included, these items should be available upon request from NSF.
h. What assumptions were made when developing your models? How have you validated these assumptions?

FIGURE 9-1 Commercialization plan outline for the new technology.

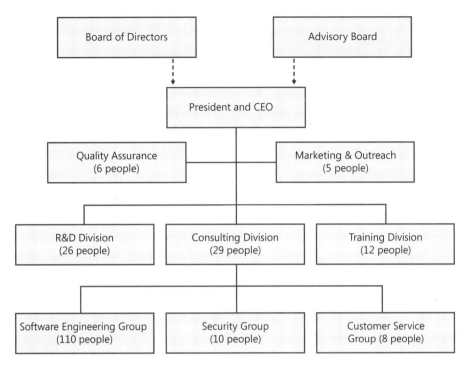

FIGURE 9-2 Small business organizational chart.

Project

As noted, the project being funded by the government customer is aimed at commercializing the active-defense technology. The twin goals of the project are to make a product from the technology and get it used by a defense project. The aim is to showcase the use of the product with the aim of interesting other defense projects in the use of the technology.

Based on your discussions with potential users, the maturity of the technology can be rated using Technology Readiness Levels (TRLs),[4] which are displayed in Table 9-1 as Level 7, a system prototype demonstration in an operational environment. Potential users say that a technology must be Level 7 or higher for them to consider it for operational use because of the risks involved.

Even though this rating scheme seems very hardware-oriented, you believe that you can still work with it to assess the technology's readiness level. You ask around to see whether there is a rating process for potential technology users. What you would like to do is assess their readiness to adopt the technology. You search the literature and make inquiries. Although your searches prove fruitless, you still think it is a good idea. Perhaps this can be a future research project?

TABLE 9-1 Technology readiness levels in the Department of Defense.

Technology Readiness Level	Description
1. Basic principles observed and reported	Lowest level of technology readiness. Scientific research begins to be translated into applied research and development. An example is paper studies of a technology's basic properties.
2. Technology concept and/or application formulated	Invention begins. Once basic principles are observed, practical applications can be invented. The application is speculative, and there is no proof or detailed analysis to support the assumption. Examples are still limited to paper studies.
3. Analytical and experimental critical function and/or characteristic proof of concept	Active research and development is initiated. This includes analytical and laboratory studies to physically validate analytical predictions or separate elements of the technology. Examples include components that are not yet integrated or representative.
4. Component and/or breadboard validation in laboratory environment	Basic technological components are integrated to establish that the pieces will work together. This is low fidelity compared to the eventual system. Examples include integration of ad hoc hardware in a laboratory.
5. Component and/or breadboard validation in relevant environment	Fidelity of breadboard technology increases significantly. The basic technological components are integrated with reasonably realistic supporting elements so that the technology can be tested in a simulated environment. Examples include a high-fidelity laboratory environment or a simulated operational environment.
6. System/subsystem model or prototype demonstration in a relevant environment	Representative model or prototype system, which is well beyond the breadboard tested for TRL 5, is tested in a relevant environment. This represents a major step up in a technology's demonstrated readiness. Examples include testing of a prototype in a high-fidelity laboratory environment or in a simulated operational environment.
7. System prototype demonstration in an operational environment	Prototype that works near or at the planned operational system level. This represents a major step up from TRL 6, requiring the demonstration of an actual system prototype in an actual operational environment. Examples include testing the prototype in a test bed.
8. Actual system completed and qualified through test and demonstration	Technology has been proven to work in its final form and under expected conditions. In almost all cases, this TRL represents the end of true system development. Examples include developmental test and evaluation of the system to determine if it meets design specifications.
9. Actual system is proven through use in successful mission operations	Actual application of the technology in its final form and under mission conditions, such as those encountered in operational test and evaluation. In almost all cases, this is the end of the last bug-fixing aspects of true system development. Examples include using the system under operational mission conditions.

Process

You have three project leaders interested in operational use of your technology. Two of the projects are for military customers, while the other involves commercial application. All three of these projects require their networks to be operational 24 hours a day/7 days a week (24/7), with at most an hour of downtime per month for planned maintenance. Before these project leaders will commit to using the technology, they plan to require that a technology readiness assessment be performed. They do this to evaluate the risks and benefits associated with the use of the technology. They each put one of their senior technical leads on a team to perform this assessment. The key output of the assessment is the impact analysis. In the case of network protection technologies like active defense, assessors look at the potential positive and negative impacts of using the technology in terms of functionality, downtime, and potential to be compromised during an attack.

As the assessment team performs their impact analysis, you try to entice them further into committing to the use of the technology by using matching funds. You also show them your initial pilot results and your commercialization plan, and you have them talk with your gambling partner to raise their level of confidence in your technology. You even conduct several demonstrations to convince them that the potential benefits of using the technology are worth the risks.

Product

You are thrilled when you learn that the assessment team reports finding that the positive impacts associated with use of the technology merit the risks involved. However, only one of the projects is at a stage where the program manager for this military project is willing to commit to partnering with you and using the technology. In return, he wants your commitment regarding the packaging of the technology so that the product will be in a form acceptable for his team's use operationally. Such packaging involves your agreeing to the following terms and conditions of use:

- Under no circumstances will you provide information about the technology to anyone outside of the project once it is perfected for use on the project. He explains that his staff has classified inputs about threats that might force you to change your algorithms in terms of the design of criteria to find the best solution. This means that you will either have to terminate your relationship with your commercial partner or develop two versions of the technology: one for the military, and the other for commercial usage. While this is doable, managing two separate commercialization paths for the technology adds cost and a degree of difficulty to the effort.

- In addition to the promised documentation, you will also generate a maintenance manual for use by project personnel when updating the toolset and the platform it resides on. You will also pay for licenses for the platform software and commercial off-the-shelf (COTS) tools that are part of the toolset.

- You will conduct two training classes for project personnel in the theory and use of the technology. These will be hands-on workshops lasting at least a week each.

- You will develop and maintain a website that facilitates responses to project queries and problem reports associated with the use of the technology within a 30-minute time period. This site will be operational 24 hours a day/7 days a week (24/7).

- You will fund the entire project. The program manager for the military partner project explains that he does not have any discretionary funds available to commit to the effort.

People

The players involved in the decision on whether to use or not to use the new technology include the following people:

- **You**   The technology developer and primary advocate for its use.

- **Your customer**   The government organization that has been sponsoring both the R&D and commercialization of the technology.

- **The program manager for the partner project**   The potential commercialization agent for the technology within the military who will take the active-defense product operational.

Even though your commercial partner in the gambling firm seems not to have any say, he is impacted by the decision. His firm has made a substantial investment, and he says that he will take legal action if you decide to not permit him to use the technology in the future.

Options, recommendations, and reactions

You, your government customer for the technology development, and the military's program manager for the potential partner project meet to discuss the possibility of pursuing a joint effort. While you do not like the partner project's terms, you are willing to accept all of them except the exclusivity clause so that you can move the technology forward the next step. However, your government customer is not willing to pay the full bill for moving the technology forward via the partner project. He wants the partner project to ante up at least a token amount of money to show its commitment. However, the program manager for the partner project is just as obstinate, saying that he has no money to put up and that you should be willing to accept his terms because he and his staff will incur most of the risk. A stalemate is reached and nobody seems willing to make a compromise.

Outcomes and lessons learned

The situation looks dire until your boss walks into the room and suggests that all three of you look at the options and develop a solution. He wants you to brief him on the options within the next week. You have no alternative but to try to solve the problem because your boss called his counterparts in the other organizations and forced the issue. You meet several times with the program manager and the government representative and develop a response for your bosses. The content of the briefing is summarized in Table 9-2. While the three of you have not reached agreement on a recommendation, you do concur that the table represents the current feasible set of options. You do not part friends. However, working together definitely eased the tension and made you see that your differences in positions were not that great.

TABLE 9-2 Potential options and their assessment.

Options	Strengths	Weaknesses
Provide the military partner exclusive use.	Keeps the technology safe from bad guys.	Limits the potential commercial use of technology.
Maintain separate military and commercial versions of the technology.	Permits commercialization while safeguarding the algorithms from potentially being compromised.	Must manage the firewalls between the two versions of the technology. The technology might evolve differently.
Sponsor funds the entire effort for the military partner.	Partner funds are dedicated to the primary mission.	No commitment is shown for commercializing the technology.
Sponsor funds the development of manuals and conducts training for the military partner.	Manual is needed, anyhow. Training can be perfected through trial use.	Additional funds are needed to accomplish both tasks. Also, this option diverts resources.
Sponsor funds a dedicated website that is operational 24/7 and provides 30-minute response times.	Provides prompt attention and solutions to problems encountered operationally.	Seems like overkill. Moving to a single shift 7 days a week cuts costs by one third.
Do nothing.	Safe and no cost.	Technology stays on the shelf and the investment lost.

The briefing is given to your boss in a very tense atmosphere. The program manager for the partner project will not change his position regarding the funding. All other issues seem negotiable. Your government customer will also not budge. He says that the military partner must put up some funds, no matter how small, to show some level of commitment. He will find the funds to handle the other issues if this one is addressed. When your boss says that he will elevate the issue to a higher authority, the partner project's program manager walks out of the meeting. As he leaves the room, he says, "I will not be forced to pay a cent, and my boss will support me." Everyone seems unhappy with this turn of events. "Do not worry," your boss says. "I can convince his boss to ante up at least a token amount by trading on past relationships."

The lessons learned in this large defense project were many and include, but are not limited to, the following:

■ Many technologies do not get adopted because of the wrong reasons. Inertia, politics, personalities, and the resistance to trying something new often get in the way.

■ Even when the benefits are large, getting an organization to adopt a new technology is a difficult undertaking. An approach is to make the rewards (financial, personal, competitive, or other) associated with technology use large enough to stimulate risk-taking. Planning for the application of change-management practices, tailored to the project phase, can help alleviate adoption problems.

■ A good way to represent technology maturity is by determining its TRL. Any of the many TRL models in use today can be employed to handle this task. My advice is to use the one your customer employs to ease any communications gap.

■ Recognize that military managers are much more conservative in their decisions than commercial managers. The military emphasizes the use of proven technology for a reason. Lives and livelihoods are at stake if the technology is immature and fails in the field.

- Use actual results whenever possible to gain momentum to get a technology adopted for widespread use. Such results should be generated on representative projects operating in as realistic an environment as possible to be deemed creditable.

- Do not forget that you need to expend the effort to make a product of the technology for adoption by prospective customers. This involves building the tools to make the technology easy to understand and use, especially when the innovation is mathematically based.

- As you commercialize a technology, you need to create the support base (manuals, training, user support, help desks, websites, and other items) required to sustain the technology in the field.

- Partnering with potential users is a good approach, especially when it requires all parties to make commitments. Both cash and noncash (in-kind investments of equipment, facilities, or people) contributions can be counted when tallying the sums.

- When people get backed into corners, they react in irrational ways. In our case, the people involved dug in their heels and held fast to their positions. Instead, some form of mediation should have been used as the briefing was crafted to try getting all parties involved to agree to a compromise.

Summary

This chapter provides you with insights into how to assess a technology's level of maturity using Technology Readiness Levels and how to engage prospective partners in commercialization activities. The major issue in technology use is always its ability to stand up to operational and environmental constraints. That is why most technology transfer experts[5] recommend conducting trials with the technology in as representative an environment as possible prior to attempting a widespread transition and operational use. This chapter emphasized risk-taking with technology when the benefits are large enough to justify it. For example, your firm might take larger risks with technology if you are lagging the industry and need to make a large jump to stay alive.

References

References cited within this chapter include the following:

[1] Constantinos Daskalakis, Rafael Frongillo, Christos H. Papadimitriou, George Pierrakos, and Gregory Valiant, "On Learning Algorithms for Nash Equilibria." See the following paper: *http://www.cs.berkeley.edu/~georgios/papers/learning.pdf*.

[2] Mike Cohn, *Succeeding with Agile: Software Development Using Scrum* (Addison-Wesley, 2009).

[3] National Science Foundation, outline of a commercialization plan, see *http://www.nsf.gov/eng/iip/sbir/commplan06.htm*.

4 Department of Defense, *Technology Readiness Assessment (TRA) Deskbook*. See *http://www.dod. gov/ddre/doc/DoD_TRA_July_2009_Read_Version.pdf*.

5 Phyllis L. Speser, *The Art and Science of Technology Transfer* (John Wiley & Sons, 2006).

Web resources

Applicable web resources that amplify points in this chapter can be found here:

- The site that I believe covers Technology Readiness Levels (TRLs) best is Wikipedia. It identifies all of the models used and describes them well at the following site: *http://en.wikipedia.org/ wiki/Technology_readiness_level*.

- The National Technology Transfer Center mission is to commercialize technologies developed by the government. More information on the resource and how it accomplishes its job can be found at *http://www.nttc.edu*.

- The Federal Laboratory Consortium for Technology Transfer maintains links to all sorts of resources on the topic of technology transfer at *http://www.federallabs.org/resources*.

- An interesting site in Canada looks at licensing technology across the university, government, and industry: *http://lesusacanada.org/MainNav/Member-Groups/Sectors/Industry-Government-Interface.aspx*.

- A government site that stresses the use of partnerships in technology transfer can be found at *http://www.ornl.gov/adm/partnerships*. Although the site is not software-oriented, it still can stimulate ideas on how to get commitment from others.

- The Association of University Technology Managers maintains an interesting site with resources, publications, blogs, and e-groups at *http://www.autm.net/Home.htm*.

- The University of Michigan provides resources for start-up ventures and entrepreneurs at the following site: *http://www.techtransfer.umich.edu/resources/venturecenter/index.php*.

- The Technology Transfer Society hosts an annual conference on the topic. Information on the 2011 conference can be found at *http://www.t2s-augsburg.com/*.

- A useful monthly newsletter on technology transfer topics is published by the Tech Transfer University at *http://www.technologytransfertactics.com*.

CHAPTER 10

Government Case: Maintenance Shop in Turmoil

Setting the stage

Your software life-cycle support center was selected two years ago to provide software maintenance and support for a transport modernization effort. There were six centers vying for the responsibility, which would result in about 100 new jobs being filled for the next 20 years. You were surprised that your center was chosen because it was the smallest, least accessible, and least able to handle the workload. The largest software maintenance project that your center has had responsibility for in the last ten years had a peak staff of 12 people. In addition, although your processes are Capability Maturity Model Integration (CMMI) Level 3, they are aimed at small projects—as is the infrastructure you use to manage them and their associated products. However, your proposal had the support of two powerful senators, five Congressmen and women, and three large local defense contractors who lobbied for you on Capitol Hill. Their support helped your center get the job, and the contractors' marketing representatives hardly let a day go by without reminding your boss of this fact.

For the past two years you have been meeting with government and contractor personnel to get ready for the transition. The prime contractor will continue to maintain the aircraft airframe and engines for the foreseeable future, as will the subcontractor who developed the Global Positioning System (GPS) navigation subsystem (both the hardware and software). You will take over responsibility for the rest of the software, which includes the overall mission, the communications, and the Heads-Up Display (HUD) packages. To ease into the role of maintenance, your center has developed a transition plan and hired 10 new employees out of core funds to get ready to take over responsibility for the project. You have also identified 22 new hires you will try to bring on as soon as you get the go-ahead from Human Resources personnel. In addition, some long-lead facilities and equipment have been acquired and configured as a System Integration Laboratory (SIL) in anticipation of your center assuming the software maintenance role. However, budgets for the transition have been slim, and actual funds for the project will not be authorized until the transition officially begins at the start of the next fiscal year, which is next month. There is a lot of work to get done in a short time, and there are few resources available to perform the tasks.

Organization

An organizational chart for the software life-cycle support center is displayed in Figure 10-1. This software organization currently has a staff of 120 professionals supporting 15 projects on a level-of-effort basis, using a mix of project-specific and core funding. There are currently 612 transports in the fleet that are deployed to 72 sites worldwide. As noted in the figure, the center is structured to use project dollars to fund maintenance or enhancement tasks and to use core budgets to address sustaining engineering activities. Because these funding lines have different restrictions on what their money can buy, mixing budgets would be counterproductive.

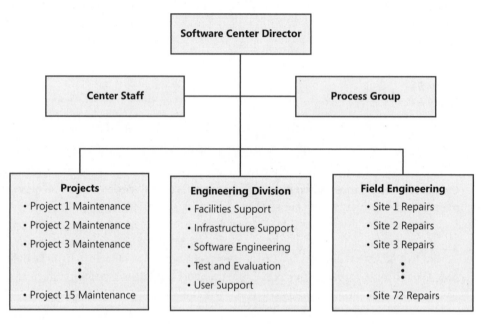

FIGURE 10-1 Software life-cycle support center organizational chart.

The software maintenance tasks for the new transport will be conducted to update the current software baseline on a periodic basis to incorporate enhancements, repair faults, and optimize performance.[1] As such, this software maintenance effort will address change requests that are made, approved, prioritized, and funded by users for a new release that is being developed and fielded, typically on an annual basis. In contrast, sustaining engineering activities[2] are those required and funded by core budgets to sustain the infrastructure, facilities, and releases in the field. Sustaining engineering will support, but be not limited to, tasks like facilities support (platform updates, COTS package updates, and so on), field engineering (such as software emergency repairs), user support (handholding, help desk, training, website support, and so on), and infrastructure tasks (configuration management, network administration, product distribution, security, and other such items).

Note that once the new transport is fielded there will be typically at least four versions of the software baseline in maintenance[2] at any one point in time. The development version represents the work in progress. This version will handle the enhancements and repairs that are being made to the software configuration for eventual delivery to the transport fleet. The fielded and in-transition versions of the software represent finished products that might need to be supported and updated to keep them operational. Finally, a requirements version is also being developed to ensure that the right changes are made in the future to ensure mission success.

Project

As previously noted, this is the biggest project your center has ever been tasked to handle. The first thing that you do as project manager is determine whether you need to alter the organization structure to support getting the job done. To make this determination, you develop the Work Breakdown Structure (WBS) illustrated in Table 10-1 based on a maintenance template developed by the U.S. Army[3] to identify the tasks you will have to tackle once turnover and transition occur. Based on the tasking, you identify the following changes that need to be accomplished for you to perform your job better:

- Because of the size of the project, report its progress directly to the director of the Software Engineering Center. This move will ensure that you have the director's ear.

- Create a dedicated project office to manage the project, with staff from functional organizations reporting to it and functional management on a parallel basis. Staff the project office with 12 people to maintain oversight on both internal and contracted efforts.

- Create a sustaining engineering division to provide the skills to perform these tasks, and move the facilities, infrastructure, and user-support functions under engineering there.

- Create an independent test and evaluation group to provide skills to perform these tasks, and move the staff from engineering there.

- Broaden the scope of the process group to encompass both process and product assurance, and rename it the *product assurance group*.

TABLE 10-1 Operations and maintenance Work Breakdown Structure.

Activity	Task	Brief Description
1.1	Maintenance	Records the costs for updating and repairing elements of the system.
1.1.1	Release Requirements	Summarizes the costs associated with release requirements formulation based on user-request and problem analysis.
1.1.2	Release Planning	Records the costs associated with developing plans, budgets, and schedules for block releases.
1.1.3	Architecture Analysis	Summarizes the costs for architecture analysis and design actions aimed at satisfying the requirements.
1.1.4	Software Defect Repair	Records the costs for repairing software defects. Such costs include engineering and testing.
1.1.5	Software Enhancements	Summarizes the costs associated with developing software enhancements and making perfective changes.
1.1.6	Release Integration and Test	Records the costs for an acceptance test of the release, including the costs associated with integration and verification.

Activity	Task	Brief Description
1.1.7	Release Delivery and Qualification	Summarizes the costs for release qualification and delivery, including those related to product release and documentation.
1.2	Sustaining Engineering	Records the costs associated with sustaining operations in the field. It includes the costs of analyses and studies, emergency repairs, and user handholding and support.
1.2.1	Analyses and Studies	Summarizes the costs associated with the conduct of analyses stemming from operational issues and problems.
1.2.2	Emergency Repairs	Records the costs related to emergency repairs, including those for development and delivery of patch releases to the field.
1.2.3	User Training	Summarizes the costs associated with providing mentoring and training.
1.2.4	External Support	Records the costs related to providing user, customer, and other forms of external support that are needed for operational testing.
1.3	Independent Test and Verification	Summarizes the costs associated with independently verifying and validating the system as releases are prepared and released. Such verification activities can range from independent testing to detailed analysis of both designs and code on a test bench.
1.3.1	Test Planning	Records the costs related to preparing test plans.
1.3.2	Test Preparation	Summarizes the costs related to developing test cases and scenarios, and the related test tools needed to run them.
1.3.3	Test Conduct	Records the costs associated with conducting the tests, capturing results, verifying that release requirements are satisfied, and developing regression test baselines for use in revalidating the system when future changes are made.
1.3.4	Independent Analysis and Verification	Records the costs related to performing the analysis of designs and code needed to provide confirmation that requirements, including those for security and safety, have been satisfied.
1.4	Product Support	Summarizes the costs associated with maintaining the overall quality of the processes, products, and supplier networks used by the system in operations, maintenance, and support.
1.4.1	Configuration Management (CM)	Records the costs associated with configuration management, including those related to Change Control Board (CCB) operations and tracking configurations, and licenses among various operational sites.
1.4.2	Quality Assurance (QA)	Summarizes the QA costs aimed at ensuring the quality and integrity of the processes used for maintenance and support.
1.4.3	Peer Reviews	Records the costs associated with conduct of peer reviews on the project, including the disposition of issues found.
1.4.4	Supplier Management	Summarizes the costs related to maintaining a liaison with suppliers, including those that provide software licenses.
1.4.5	Security	Records the costs associated with security, including those related to security such as planning, training, and controls.
1.5	Information Assurance	Summarizes the costs related to information assurance, including those associated with product and computer network protection.

Activity	Task	Brief Description
1.5.1	Protection Services	Records the costs associated with product protection, including any associated with maintaining any Secure Compartmented Information Facilities (SCIFs).
1.6	Acquisition Support	Summarizes the costs associated with providing oversight and support for acquisition-management activities. Such costs often occur when managing third parties doing maintenance activities.
1.7	Operations Support	Records the costs associated with supporting operations in the field, including those costs associated with database maintenance, configuration, and system administration.
1.8	Facility Support	Summarizes the costs needed to ready and maintain the development and test facilities needed to maintain and sustain the system in the field.
1.8.1	Maintenance Facility Sustainment	Summarizes the costs related to readying and maintaining a maintenance facility that can be used to develop and sustain the system once it is fielded.
1.8.2	SIL Sustainment	Records the costs associated with readying and maintaining a System Integration Laboratory (SIL) that is used to test new releases destined for the field under realistic operating conditions.
1.8.3	Equipment Sustainment	Records costs associated with setting up and keeping tactical hardware used in the SIL operational.
1.8.4	Network Operations and Administration	Summarizes the costs associated with managing and maintaining the networks used for maintaining, operating, and supporting the system.
1.9	Field Support	Records the costs of conducting field support, including both labor and travel components.
1.10	Management	Records the costs related to managing release and sustaining-engineering activities and conducting metrics analyses.
1.10.1	Release Management	Summarizes the costs associated with managing the generation of releases.
1.10.2	Sustaining Engineering Management	Records the costs related to managing the sustaining-engineering efforts for the system, including those associated with independent testing; independent verification; acquisition, product, field, and facility support; and information assurance.
1.10.3	Risk Management	Summarizes the costs associated with planning for and performing risk-management activities on the project.
1.10.4	Measurement Analysis	Records the costs associated with the collection, analysis, and reporting of measurement data.
1.11	Licenses	Summarizes the costs for software licenses.
1.12	Contractual Capability Set FY	Records the costs for acquiring a software contractual capability set across a number of designated fiscal years. These costs include the following: ■ Troubleshoot/correct issues ■ Cyclic release of new/revised versions ■ Respond to new threats or requirements ■ Maintain interoperability with other changing systems ■ Accommodate new weapons, systems, or munitions ■ Increase efficiency/effectiveness ■ Support new doctrine/tactics ■ Ensure compatibility with replacement COTS ■ Satisfy policy mandates ■ Address affordability concerns

Process

You have a great deal of work ahead according to the WBS in Table 10-1. Although you had processes on the books in the past, much of this work was done in an ad hoc way on a project. For example, you brought in a specialist from the infrastructure support group who understood and helped you with the change-control process when you needed configuration management help. Now you'll need to have your staff ramp up the change-control processes and tailor them for use on the project. You'll also need to interface these processes and the tools that automate them with those being used by the contractors, because you are responsible for maintaining the software baselines. This project presents you with a totally different ballgame.

Of course, you will use the center's institutional processes as your basis. But there are lots of decisions to be made regarding how you are going tailor them for use. Many processes need to be beefed up because they were designed for small projects. The organization is especially weak in the following six CMMI[4] process areas:

- **Maturity Level 2** Project Planning (PP), Process Monitoring and Control (PMC), Measurement and Analysis (MA), and Configuration Management (CM)

- **Maturity Level 3** Integrated Project Management (IPM) and Risk Management (RSKM).

The process group lead has agreed to address these weaknesses and come back to you with recommendations. You are afraid that the group lead will view this as an opportunity to bleed the project financially to solve larger organizational issues that surfaced as a result of an appraisal that was recently held in anticipation of moving to CMMI Maturity Level 4. You will have to be careful.

Product

One of biggest issues facing you is configuring versions of products for distribution to the field and qualifying them for aircraft use. Because the transport fleet is currently in use by all three branches of the armed services (as well as by the National Guard), the software will have to be generated and distributed to the field from your updated baseline. Each version of the software will have to be tested separately both in the SIL and in the field prior to qualification via flight testing. The challenges in integration and testing are many and unlike those experienced during development. In recent studies, it was found that the activity distributions,[5] as illustrated in Figure 10-2, during maintenance differ greatly from those experienced during development. Work performed tends to be heavily test-focused rather than requirements-oriented. The reason for this is because the software baseline must be requalified each time changes have been made to it.

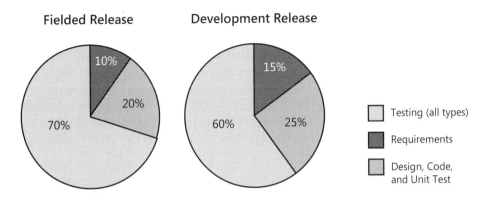

Fielded Release

10%
20%
70%

Development Release

15%
25%
60%

Testing (all types)

Requirements

Design, Code,
and Unit Test

FIGURE 10-2 Distribution of product-release activities in fielded and development versions.

People

Another issue is related to staffing the project. Not only is getting the large numbers of people required difficult, so are the skills required. Hiring anyone via the civil service system in the United States is neither speedy nor easy. Positions must be advertised and competed for before they can be awarded—especially for middle and upper grades, which are the center's need. Salaries in government are typically lower than those in commercial industry. As a consequence, hiring from outside is also difficult, even though government jobs are looked at as more stable.

The belief that junior staff can and should perform software maintenance is also wrong. They just do not have the skills and experience to do the job properly. Again, according to recent studies,[5] those performing maintenance tasks tend to be software professionals with over ten years of know-how rather than developers with less than half of that experience. These performers come to the table with skills, knowledge, and ability that are vastly superior to those who have just entered the workforce, especially when working with real-time embedded systems.

The dilemma is that you will be hiring many people other than software engineers. Many of these new people will also fill positions that have never existed before at the center. For example, although software testing will be done by the software engineers, system integration and testing will be the responsibility of the test and evaluation department. To accomplish this, testers will need a different skill set and different abilities. For instance, they will have to write end-to-end scenarios to play against the system as it is being integrated to determine whether or not it responds to real-time stimuli. In response to these needs, you have to prepare position descriptions for these jobs before your personnel department will start its search for candidates. This is a labor-intensive task that must be accomplished immediately to get the ball rolling, as the need for personnel during startup is a critical success factor.

Options, recommendations, and reactions

Again, there is so much to do and so little time. Management understands and wants to help. They ask you to meet with them and tell them what you need to be successful. This is your big chance to get started in the right direction. For the meeting, you decide to prepare a Top 10 list in the form of the risk matrix shown in Table 10-2 to highlight your immediate needs and provide an impact justification for the project at this point in time in its life cycle—startup. When requesting help, you use the concept of controllables versus noncontrollables, which one of your first bosses taught you to use when requesting assistance on items outside of your immediate span of control as a project manager. These are the items that management can help you with the most.

TABLE 10-2 Top 10 risk matrix and impact assessment.

Risk	Need Description	Impact Assessment
1. Staffing: government personnel system is too hard to use and takes too long	Have personnel use expedited request-processing overrides.	Without proper staffing, we will not be able to deliver the first release per the agreed-to schedule.
2. Staffing: needed to handle peaks and valleys	Hire a firm to provide qualified contract personnel.	Acts as a contingency plan in case the staffing plan above fails.
3. Get an adequate budget authorized for startup	Have funds incrementally allocated annually to the project on a level-of-effort basis, assuming fixed staff counts. In other words, staff levels and schedules are fixed, and there is no flexibility to vary either.	Startup funding is 20% higher than normal. Without added funds, not all tasks can be performed. This means some changes/repairs will have to be postponed until the next release.
4. Authorize a training budget for the project	Use project money for training because the core funding shortfall does not cover project needs.	Improve productivity by addressing learning-curve issues on a just-in-time basis.
5. Realign the process to reflect the actual project workload	Realign the process to address maintenance tasks in the WBS.	Improve productivity by aligning the process with the work.
6. Provide office space, and co-locate personnel	Move staff into the co-located space in buildings 423 and 424. Move other staff to building 231.	Improve productivity by improving communications and teamwork.
7. Speed up equipment purchases	Accelerate the approval process with purchasing for SIL equipment.	Suppress delays in the startup because equipment is late.
8. Speed up licensing	Accelerate the legal review and purchasing for software licenses.	Suppress delays in the startup because licenses are pending.
9. Ready the SIL	Authorize the use of capital funds to ready the SIL for use. Requires major facility modifications.	Suppress delays in the startup because facilities are not ready when needed.
10. Contractor information access	Put enabling clauses in contracts to permit the center staff to access contractor information.	Make it difficult to integrate contractor deliveries with software release baselines.

You also need help with some of the institutional systems because they are not set up to support a project of this size. The worst of these is your timecard and accounting system. Charge numbers are typically allocated for a project with no clear visibility into work packages at the subtask level (software development instead of design, code, unit checkout, and so forth of either components or releases). Accounting is done monthly, with paper reports being published two weeks later. This is a known problem that management hopes the planned move to a new timecard and accounting system will correct. However, the move has been delayed several times, and there is a great deal of resistance to the change. Project managers have argued against the move because of the added burden such accounting would place on them as managers of small projects.

Outcomes and lessons learned

The meeting with management went well. You set the agenda and got them talking about things they could do that actually could help you get the job done. But they admitted there were systems used by the government that even they could not influence. The personnel, timecard, and accounting systems fit into this category. In response, the following list summarizes the actions they took to address your Top 10 risks:

- Will have Human Resources personnel use expedited requests to fill your personnel vacancies.

- The center already has an arrangement with a firm to supply contract labor. Will put enabling clauses in the contract to allow you to fill vacancies on a short-term basis.

- They cannot address the budgeting cycle because funds are allocated by a higher authority to the command and then to the center. This is the way the government does business.

- Authorizing the project budget for training is a no-brainer. They approve the request immediately at the meeting.

- Because the process group is down to one person, management says they will agree to realign the process if you agree to put two project-funded people on the task full time for six months.

- They agree that you need office space. However, it will be about a year before they can act because the buildings in question are scheduled for refurbishment within the next year.

- They will try to put some pressure on the legal and purchasing departments to speed up equipment purchases and licensing. But it will have to be done gently; otherwise, those departments might respond negatively and put your purchase requests on the bottom of the pile.

- They cannot address the facility issues now. Funds have finally arrived after a five-year wait for renovation, and nobody in the management chain wants to put the funds in jeopardy.

- Putting the enabling clause in the contract should be easy. Management will request that the acquisition office responsible for the contract do this, and they will follow through to ensure that the request is acted upon.

All in all, you did well. The lessons learned in this maintenance project were many and include, but are not limited to, the following:

- The work that must be completed as part of the software maintenance effort is much different than just updating and repairing the development-software baseline. In the case of many large projects, there may be sustaining engineering, acquisition management, and test and evaluation tasks that need to be performed that are just as important as the update job.

- To succeed with maintenance in most organizations, you must define what work has to be done, when it must be done, how it must be done, and who does it. Then you must fight for the many types of resources (staff, money, space, equipment, facilities, and other key items) needed to get the job done, typically on a level-of-effort basis over the course of a year. In other words, staff levels are fixed, as are schedules.

- Maintenance organizations set up for handling small projects might have to be changed when large projects are encountered. The primary reason for this is that communications patterns differ as the workforce is increased to handle the work flow across the organization.

- Processes established for development projects need to be enhanced to address the additional needs of maintenance groups for broadened coverage. For example, configuration-management processes need to be expanded to address distribution control because releases, once qualified, are often sent to hundreds of sites in different configurations.

- Using the concept of controllables and noncontrollables is powerful because it allows you to understand what you can and cannot do within your limited span of control.

- Institutional barriers are the most difficult to confront early in a project. Resolving these at least partially can make life easier, especially if you work for an organization where such barriers interfere with your ability to get the job done.

- Those trying to get things done in government organizations face many unique obstacles. Many of these barriers were created because someone did something wrong in the past and a set of checks and balances was needed to ensure such mistakes were not made in the future.

Summary

This chapter focuses on the work that needs to be done during software maintenance and the organizational changes needed to accomplish them. The major issues encountered during maintenance arise because the resources provided to accomplish this work are typically allocated on a level-of-effort basis for a fixed time period. This means that the only way to accommodate cost growth is to defer changes and repairs to later releases. The case also stresses the need to tackle the issues you can control and ask for help on the others.

References

References cited within this chapter include the following:

[1] IEEE Std. 1219-1998, *IEEE Standard for Software Maintenance,* Institute of Electrical and Electronics Engineers (IEEE), 1998.

[2] Donald J. Reifer, *Software Maintenance Success Recipes* (Auerbach, 2011).

[3] Donald J. Reifer, Cheryl Jones, James Judy, and Jeramia Poland, *Software Operations, Maintenance and Support Work Breakdown Structure, Version 1.4,* U.S. Army, December 2010.

[4] Dennis A. Ahern, Aaron Clouse, and Richard Turner, *CMMI Distilled* (Addison-Wesley, 2001).

[5] Donald J. Reifer, Jill Ann Allen, Brian Fersch, Barbara Hitchings, James Judy, and Wilson Rosa, "Software Maintenance: Debunking the Myths," *Proceedings of ISPA/SCEA Conference,* 2009.

Web resources

Applicable web resources that amplify points made in this chapter can be found here:

- Amazon provides links to the current software maintenance literature at *www.amazon.com.*

- The Data & Analysis Center for Software provides pointers to a wealth of software maintenance resources at *http://www.thedacs.com/databases/url/key/5881.*

- A good bibliography of software maintenance books is available at the following site: *http://users.jyu.fi/~koskinen/bibsmb.htm.*

- Software-supportability.org provides articles on this important topic and on reliability at *http://www.software-supportability.org.*

- The Journal of Software Maintenance and Evolution, Research and Practice provides some interesting articles on maintenance topics, mainly from universities, at the following site: *http://onlinelibrary.wiley.com/journal/10.1002/(ISSN)1532-0618.*

- The Software Engineering Maintenance and Evolution Research Unit (College of William and Mary) is pursuing some interesting research on maintenance topics, which is described at *http://www.cs.wm.edu/semeru.*

- Of course, I would be remiss in not recommending my own site, which contains some useful pointers to software maintenance information at *www.reifer.com/.*

CHAPTER 11

Academic Case: Establishing a Meaningful Collaboration with Industry

Setting the stage

You run a firm that sells software packages that estimate the cost of construction for various types of buildings. This commercial software is licensed by thousands of companies on an annual basis and comes with updates, training, and support. Your firm has been in business for over a decade and makes a good profit. Because your family owns a construction firm, you grew up in the business. Since you were a kid, you have been working around construction sites and warehouses as a laborer, driver, carpenter, plumber, electrician, and foreman. You worked your way through high school and college on construction jobs and capitalized on this experience. You therefore understand the construction business from the inside out and know what it is like to get your hands dirty.

In high school, you decided to combine your knowledge of construction and passion for programming into your own small business. As a student, you selected, acquired, installed, and made new accounting and billing software for your family's firm. During this process, you found that you could add an inventory module that minimized the amount of supplies your family kept on hand in the warehouse. This software saved your family's firm thousands of dollars, and you could use it to keep its inventory under control. You no longer needed to buy and keep piles and piles of construction supplies on hand for the next job. Instead, the software you designed could order needed supplies on a just-in-time basis. Besides helping with supplies, this practice also helped reduce inventory taxes.

Your family suggested that you contact the software vendor and sell your inventory software to them because of the success the firm was having. With your parents' help, you negotiated an agreement with the software vendor that paid you a royalty for every sale they made of your software. Your dad's lawyer helped you with the agreement, and the money started rolling in. However, the situation soured shortly afterwards as the software vendor developed its own competing package and stopped selling yours.

In college, you majored in computer science as an undergraduate. However, you continued to work part time in the office of your family's firm to pay tuition and earn spending money. You loved college and excelled in your classes. You also dabbled in developing other software packages for the construction business. But, after being burned in a business deal during high school, you were wary about partnering with others to market and sell these packages. In your senior year, you incorporated a small software business as a Limited Liability Corporation (LLC). You set up a website and sold several packages to interested parties online, earning a few thousand dollars a month in this manner.

In your senior year, you also decided to continue your education in graduate school at the same university. You enrolled in the business school and pursued a degree in quantitative business analysis, which led to a Masters of Business Administration (MBA) degree. You excelled and put your classes on data analysis, probability and statistics, and mathematical modeling to work in your business. You took classes from your favorite professor, and he became your mentor.

For your thesis, you devised a new mathematical model using Bayesian statistical techniques[1] that accurately estimated the cost of construction projects. Bayesian techniques allowed you to take advantage of market knowledge to predict the future cost of materials used in construction. As part of this effort, you took advantage of your many contacts in the construction industry to gather data on past and current costs of materials for use in validating your model. Needless to say, the formulas worked extremely well. Of course, you received an "A" for your work. Your professor was thrilled by your innovation and encouraged you to publish the algorithm in the *Journal of Cost Analysis and Parametrics*.[2] He volunteered to help you write the article, which when completed was submitted, accepted, and published in this prestigious journal. Both your name and his name appeared on the publication, and you both are credited with the innovation even though his only contribution was editing and advice on getting it published.

Your plan on graduation was to take your modeling innovations to market. You believed that you could be successful with a startup company because you had the money in the bank to handle the startup costs, as well as the industry contacts and the marketing channels to pull it off. As you worked on your thesis, your professor and fellow graduate students provided lots of advice and guidance in experimental design and validation of models. Because you valued these relationships, you hired one of your fellow graduate students to work for your LLC part time and your favorite professor to act as a consultant. Per your professor's advice, you spent the time to develop a business plan and prepare a list of targets for sale of your products.

Organization

As part of your business plan, you defined the organizational structure that is pictured in Figure 11-1. While you currently have only two people and a consultant working for the firm, you structured it because you are sure that you will grow in the near future. As noted, you will be the president and CEO, head of all departments, and chief architect for your firm. Your college friend and new hire will be the chief software engineer, and the professor will be the consultant. Other positions in the organization will have to wait to be filled as sales increase and the LLC grows.

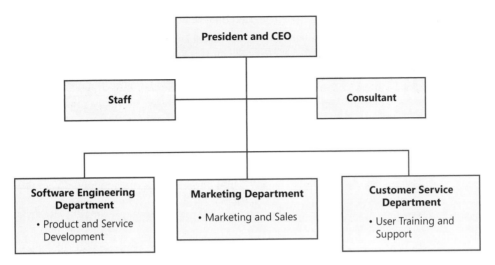

FIGURE 11-1 Future organizational chart for the LLC.

Project

You have a number of things to do to get ready before you can start selling products. Your to-do list and schedule are summarized in Table 11-1, along with a designation of who is responsible for completing each task. Because you developed a working spreadsheet version of the cost model for your thesis, you decide to update your website and get your marketing materials finished first so that you can start taking orders for the software package prior to its being released for sale. This will permit you to derive some revenue as you develop a more industrial-grade modeling package in parallel during the next six months. You also plan to update the spreadsheet once the cost model is complete and to keep it current. You will send the spreadsheet out with promotional materials to act as a sales tool to capture the interest of prospective clients.

Meanwhile, you have your employee populating the materials database with vendor prices so that users can shop around and purchase construction goods from the cheapest supplier. You believe that this feature will get potential buyers' interest and stimulate sales. You have also asked your wife and teenage daughter to help on a part-time basis by preparing the website and Internet-based documentation and helping with the online marketing. As Table 11-1 illustrates, you have developed an aggressive schedule because you want to get products to market quickly.

TABLE 11-1 To-do list and schedule for developing estimating product and services.

To-Do List	Schedule (months after start)	Responsible Person
Update website and add pizazz	1	Wife
Develop e-mail flier and product prospectus	1	You
Develop list of products and services you will offer	2	You
Develop price list for products and services	2	You
Develop potential client list, and e-mail flier to them	3	Daughter
Develop marketing support literature and presentations	3	Wife
Populate model knowledge databases, and keep current	3	Employee
Respond to inquiries, and follow up on sales leads	4 to 6	Wife and daughter
Develop production version of model	4	You
Test production version of model in family business setting	5	You
Launch product at trade fair in local area	5	You
Develop web-based model users and reference manuals	5	Employee
Develop training materials, and offer in-house courses	5	You
Develop Internet-based model calibration support service	6	You
Take stock and figure out what to do next	6	You

Process

You are working 18 hour days to finish the items on your to-do list. However, it seems like there are a thousand interruptions a day as you try to develop the product, support the marketing effort, and develop the draft documents and training materials. You find that your employee seems to need constant direction, and your wife and daughter are getting distracted by soccer and your daughter's other scheduled after-school events (including dances, chorus, and boys). You think that it might have been easier just to try to do everything all by yourself. But, as you think about it, there just is not enough time in the day to get all of the work you have outlined done by your lonesome.

You learned that process was important during graduate school. The software development process you have settled on is Agile by definition. You are developing the product in iterations and making a version public for review on a weekly basis. The professor is evaluating your code and testing the public version of each delivery to provide you with independent feedback about the package's utility and usability. But you are starting to worry about this arrangement because you are being billed about $1,000 weekly for what you consider marginal inputs. Perhaps things will get better as you make more progress. You have made a conscious effort to develop a well-architected design, code to standards, and maintain control over versions. Having the spreadsheet version helps in testing because you can compare computational results against it to determine if mathematical errors occurred in your implementation.

Product

You are a little over four months into the project, and the product is coming together nicely. However, you still have too much to do to get the product out on schedule. In addition, orders started to pour in as soon as the website went operational, and there are six construction firms in the local area that are interested enough to schedule presentations and demonstrations. When you discuss the problem with the professor, he provides you with some sound advice. He suggests that you enlist the support of one of the undergraduate teams at the university that have a software engineering project to complete as part of their 16-week capstone course in computer science this semester. This senior-level course stresses practical application of concepts learned in real-world applications. Projects are just starting, and by collaborating with the university you can get ten to twelve smart students to work with you to develop software for you for a grade rather than money. In exchange for giving them real-world experience, you get free help. This solution sounds almost too good to be true. You contact the appropriate department and sign up. The agreement you enter into with the university is relatively simple because it focuses on defining roles and responsibilities. The contract looks pretty standard to your untrained eye. Two days later, you go to the campus to brief the assembled teams on your proposed project. Your hope is that you can get one of the teams enrolled in the course to agree to pursue your product development. The start date for the class is two weeks away. You are excited to be back on campus because it radiates energy. There are about 75 students in the room vying for industry projects that include office automation, robotic control, emergency response team operations, and commercial package applications.

People

One of the teams agrees to work with you. It is made up of 12 students from six nations: one from China, four from India, two from Korea, one from Chile, one from Egypt, and three from the United States. They organize into three teams of four to do their work. The course coordinator, a graduate student from Malaysia, asks you to brief the students further on the project, its requirements, and your expectations during the following week. You prepare your materials and meet with the team as scheduled. The students seem very excited by the materials. They outline the actions that the three teams will take and a tentative schedule on the white board. However, you are somewhat taken aback by their plans because they seem to be adhering to an academic agenda relative to development. Rather than taking what you have already completed and adding to it, the first thing they want to do is develop a requirements specification for the product. It does not seem to matter that feature lists exist, performance expectations have been documented, the design has been completed, and you are well into coding. When you complain, several team members come unglued. They argue that code will fall out quickly once the requirements are baselined. While you agree in theory, the requirements and design already exist and you view the work as wasted effort. But requirements are not written down to the format that the professor has taught them to follow. They say that it will take only a couple of weeks to pull these documents together, and it is important to do so because their grade depends on it.

Because there is no retreat on their part as their grade is on the line, you compromise and agree that a two-week delay to prepare requirements and design specifications is probably worthwhile. The team then asks you to spend three hours a day for the next four days working with each of them to help define their products and set expectations. They argue that in some cases you have to take a step backward to take two steps forward. You try to schedule the meetings across different days than they pick, but they cannot accommodate this because classes interfere. Although you agree to the four sessions that they picked out, the meetings are scheduled such that you will have to juggle work that you had planned to complete and reschedule it to the weekend.

You travel to campus for the sessions. One of the students is a no-show at the first meeting. When you ask about her absence, the others state that she had scheduling conflicts and had to put her classes first. The other team members say not to worry, they will bring her up to speed. This happens again during the third team meeting. During several of the sessions, you notice that communications issues dominate because English is not the primary language of most of the team members. The team leaders who surfaced are mostly foreign. They take control based on their natural leadership skills. But the other team members seem to have problems understanding them because they are unclear and talk too fast when they get excited. To help get your points across, you slow down, repeat things, and ask those in attendance whether or not they understand. You think you have the situation under control until a question is asked that proves that you do not. You are frustrated and let the course coordinator know that before you leave on the third day when the meetings are over. She tells you to have faith and watch as the situation straightens itself out. "Grades are on the line," she says, "and the students are motivated."

Meanwhile, more orders are pouring in via your website and your employee, wife, and daughter are complaining that they need more of your time to address issues that have arisen. They have lots of questions from prospective clients about the product, its cost, and the terms of the license that you drafted. Because about half of these queries are from their "hot leads" list, they need to be answered soon or you will lose the potential sale.

You seem pulled in a hundred directions as you try to allocate time for others and delay your schedules to help them achieve theirs. Meanwhile, feedback is still being provided by the professor along with his bills even though you have not done much with the code and product development has literally stopped because you are strapped for time. While you value his inputs and coaching, the constant billing is starting to annoy you. But you do not have the nerve to approach him and ask him to stop charging you for his services. He is your mentor, and you do not want to hurt his feelings. You decide to take the easy road and continue paying him.

Options, recommendations, and reactions

You are now four months into the effort and at the point where you have to decide whether or not adding staff to a late project will make it later.[3] The semester is nearing its end, and the student project is wrapping up. Thank goodness that the only thing left for you to do is provide the course coordinator the suggested grades for the effort. When asked to show you what they did, the students provide you with the list of products in Table 11-2 to justify their grades.

Progress has picked up, but you are still worried about meeting your commitments, especially to your wife and daughter. Sales have taken off in spite of your inattention to your marketing efforts, and you have to do something soon about preparing the needed manuals and training or the clients will cancel their orders. You have 22 solid orders on the books for the software and 28 hard requests for more information that might lead to other sales. To make an assessment about what to do now, you take stock of what progress you have made during the past few months. Although a lot has been accomplished, as illustrated in Table 11-3, there still is a great deal to get done.

TABLE 11-2 Student deliverables.

Student Team	Focus	Deliverable
1	■ Requirements and design	■ Requirements specification ■ Architecture and design specification
2	■ Code and unit checkout ■ GUI design	■ Design and coding standards ■ Graphical user interface (GUI) code developed via rapid prototype, with you in the loop ■ Feedback on existing design and coding, including error reports (mostly standards violations) ■ Unit test plans and procedures
3	■ Testing	■ Overall system test plan ■ Test scenario template ■ Regression testing guidelines
4	■ Documentation	■ Draft HTML reference manual containing explanation of mathematics ■ Draft HTML users' manual (about half completed)

TABLE 11-3 Status of effort after four months.

To-Do List	Schedule	Status
Update website and add pizazz	1	Done
Develop e-mail flier and product prospectus	1	Done
Develop list of products and services you will offer	2	Done
Develop price list for products and services	2	Done
Develop potential client list, and e-mail flier to them	3	Done
Develop marketing support literature and presentations	3	Done
Populate model knowledge databases, and keep current	3	Late, awaiting your inputs
Respond to inquiries, and follow up on sales leads	4 to 6	Awaiting your inputs
Develop production version of model	4	One month late
Test production version of model in family business setting	5	One month late
Launch product at trade fair in local area	5	Use the spreadsheet because the trade fair will not wait.
Develop web-based model users and reference manuals	5	Two months late, but student work will make it easier
Develop training materials, and offer in-house courses	5	Two months late
Develop Internet-based model calibration support service	6	Two months late
Take stock and figure out what to do next	6	Whenever

Outcomes and lessons learned

Your assessment shows that you are not as bad off as you thought you were. You achieved a lot in a short period of time and are in a position to start servicing clients. In addition, the students are busy polishing up their products and have generated some worthwhile artifacts. While the skeletal product they developed for the GUI cannot be used as is, the screen designs look good and there is some code you can use to your advantage as you finish the product. The manuals are not too bad either, and you like how they inserted links so that materials are readily accessible. So their effort was not as much a waste of time as you first thought. Unfortunately, their goals and yours did not converge because they were more document-driven than code-driven in their efforts. Their lack of focus on generating code products was disappointing, as was the amount of time you had to devote to bringing them up to speed on what you were trying to accomplish. In retrospect, you probably would not have signed up for free student help if you had it to do over again because, as you found out, the help actually was not so free. Yet, the questions the students posed and the vitality they brought to the effort was invigorating at times.

After looking the situation over, you feel that there is hope. When you take stock of your situation, you find out that you are really not as far behind as you feared. You feel that you can catch up in about a month. When status queries are received, you can use the old excuse that the firm had a software problem to save face and buy time with prospective clients. After all, you have a number of solid orders for the production software on the books and sales are building steam. After much thought, you feel that you can close on the prospects for other orders if you emphasize marketing rather than production in the near-term and follow up on leads.

There were several disturbing things that happened during the last month. First, you received questions from a large, international company in the construction business about your journal article. They expressed an interest in having their people meet with you to discuss using your model. Luckily, you did not publish all of the details about the algorithms in the paper. They probably would have taken the algorithms and used them internally without contacting you because anything that is published in a journal is public information. If you want to retain control of intellectual property, your lawyer tells you, never put it in the public domain.

The second thing that occurred is the university wants to publish a "lessons learned" report about the team's experience on the project. When you try to stop them, they argue that freedom of publication rules in the university environment. Your lawyers agree and tell you that the university can publish whatever it wants to because you did not put any exclusion clauses into the agreement you signed with the Computer Science department. According to your legal advisors, the best thing you can do is try to limit the damage by having the university agree not to discuss the algorithms in its report. This is agreed to after much discussion. But to secure the compromise, you had to agree to provide the university with a free copy of your software.

The lessons learned in this university collaboration project were many and include, but are not limited to, the following:

- Universities represent an open environment that can stimulate innovation and excitement on a project. However, bringing the innovations born in such an environment to market takes initiative and a great deal of hard work.

- When something sounds too good to be true, it probably is. Getting free help from a student team sounded like a good deal at first. But the amount of time and effort required to bring them up to speed proved to be counterproductive, especially on a small project.

- Adding people to a late project often makes it later, because people already on the project have to be taken off their current tasks to bring the new people up to speed so that they can accomplish the work efforts they have been assigned.

- Not surprisingly, university and industrial projects are often at odds with one another. The reason for this is simple. University projects stress achieving experimentation and learning goals, while industrial projects emphasize product development and on-time and on-budget delivery.

- Straight talk might have stopped the professor from charging the project inappropriately and then resume his billing when the team resumed product development.

- Emphasizing marketing at the expense of product development can often backfire. Balance between the two is needed to keep clients content. Clients are often wary of vendors who continuously slip schedules and fail to satisfy their commitments and promises.

- Read agreements carefully, and always get a legal review before signing them. You will often be surprised by what these agreements do and do not contain. In this case study, the agreement reached in high school for marketing products should have included a derivative works clause. This would have made it illegal for the firm to which the idea was licensed to develop a competing product. For the startup LLC, the clause on open publications in the university agreement should have been stricken to limit any potential exposure of the idea.

- Publishing innovations in open journals is dangerous because it puts inventions into the public domain. While it is great to get recognition for ideas, such openness is often unwise because it makes it easy for others to take and use your intellectual property without them paying you for it.

- Limiting permission for publication about ideas in partner agreements is another thing to consider. In this case, university exposure of your innovation could have been avoided by simply scoping such limitations in an agreement between collaborating parties.

Summary

This chapter highlights how an idea born in a university environment progresses from inception to commercialization. The major issues that occur are related to resolving conflicts that arise when trying to get a large number of tasks done quickly with limited resources. Pressure builds as marketing and product development activities progress in parallel. Compromises have to be made in development as clients are being served, especially in a startup environment. The case identifies several additional issues that can arise when a university is employed to assist in product development. Because goals can be in conflict, getting university teams to deliver according to production schedules often proves difficult.

References

References cited within this chapter include the following:

[1] Michael Goldstein and David Wooff, *Bayes Linear Statistics: Theory & Methods* (John Wiley & Sons, 2007).

[2] *The Journal of Cost Analysis and Parametrics* is published by the Society of Cost Estimation and Analysis (SCEA). Information on the journal is available at the following site: *http://www.sceaonline.org/publications/journal.cfm*.

[3] Frederick P. Brooks, *The Mythical Man-Month* (Addison-Wesley, 1995).

Web resources

Applicable web resources that amplify points made in this chapter can be found here:

- The U.S. Small Business Administration (SBA) provides tools and resources aimed at helping startups and entrepreneurs grow small businesses at *http://www.sba.gov*.

- For a list of SBA offices, go to the following site: *http://www.sba.gov/about-offices-list/2*.

- Dunn and Bradstreet (D&B) also provides resources aimed at helping small businesses succeed, which are available at the following website: *http://www.allbusiness.com*.

- SCORE provides mentoring, workshops, templates, and tools directed toward the needs of startups at *http://www.score.org*.

- Entrepreneur's Small Business Resource Center provides information on business basics and well-written how-to guides at the following site: *http://www.entrepreneur.com/smbresourcecenter*.

- The Small Business and Technology Development Center in North Carolina publishes a resource guide that is packed with lots of information, much of which is generic enough to be useful to new startups, at *http://www.sbtdc.org/pdf/startup.pdf*.

- Not to be left out, the State of Alabama publishes another resource guide about doing business in that state at *http://www.asbdc.org/library/alanswr.pdf.*

- A helpful and comprehensive new business startup checklist can be found at either of the following two websites: *http://www.mynewcompany.com/checklist.htm* or *http://www.bsorchecklist.org.*

- There are many university programs aimed at helping startups succeed in business. One that I like is located at the University of Colorado. Information on this program can be found at *http://www.businessstartupinstitute.com.*

- There are other university programs aimed at building entrepreneurship skills, such as the one at Stanford that provides videos, podcasts, and a variety of other resources at the following site: *http://ecorner.stanford.edu.*

CHAPTER 12

Making an Impact

Secrets of success

The ten case studies in this book should provide you with a lot of food for thought about what the real issues are for those of us who are trying to make needed changes to development processes. The cases amplify the point that all barriers to change are psychological and managerial. Many of the obstacles you face seem endemic to the way organizations conduct their business.

Take our maintenance case study (the case study in Chapter 10, "Government Case: Maintenance Shop in Turmoil") as an example. Most of the challenges that the software support center faced in this situation stemmed from the way the government allocated its budgets, handled its timecards and accounting, administered its personnel, and did its contracting. The important thing to realize in this case was that such problems were outside of your immediate span of control. Yes, there were things you could do to influence the outcome. In the case study, we hired contract personnel because it was easier to get money and approval to hire contractors than fight the government personnel system. But, in this case as in reality, you cannot change the way the government does business. Only the Congress and President of the United States can accomplish this feat. And, even for them, making such changes is often not easy because many of the practices that government organizations use are founded in the law.

The previous paragraph highlights one of the major secrets of success when dealing with change that I hoped to communicate to you via our cases: address the things that you can control because these are things that you can directly influence. There are nine other such secrets, and I highlighted them for you in Table 12-1 and amplified them in the text that follows the table. I also share what I consider to be the 12 lessons learned. The difference between a *secret* and a *lesson* is that secrets act as guiding principles, while you can take lessons learned and put them to work as you make improvements. All of these secrets and lessons learned will sound trite when you first read them. You probably will say to yourself either "I knew that" or "So what?". However, I can guarantee that most of these concepts were not employed in many of the change situations I have been involved with. Therefore, I hope that you seize these "ten secrets of success" and what I call my Dirty Dozen lessons learned as the major takeaways from this book.

TABLE 12-1 Ten secrets of success when dealing with process changes.

Number	Success Secret
1	View change from multiple perspectives.
2	Emphasize change roles and defined processes as you roll out the innovation.
3	Look for the obvious and the low-hanging fruit as your first order of business.
4	Most barriers to change are psychological and behavioral.
5	Even when you think the need for change is obvious, barriers to it can pop up from the most unexpected sources.
6	Always tie change to business objectives. Then, when presenting justifications for the change, let the numbers do the talking.
7	Not all change is good. Sometimes it makes sense not to pursue it.
8	Do not lose sight of marketplace discriminators when making changes.
9	Control the controllables, and do the things that you can do.
10	Do not forget that you need to expend the effort to make a product out of the technology.

Table 12-1 provides a handy summary of the Top 10 secrets of success. The following list looks at them in a bit more detail:

- View change from multiple perspectives. As I related in Chapter 1, "Getting Started," change is neither simple to visualize nor one dimensional. That is why I suggested that you view change from at least the five viewpoints I used to scope each of the ten case studies in this volume— that is, organizational, project, process, product, and people.

- The importance of change roles and processes cannot be overemphasized. If you do not define these aspects of your change effort, people will not understand their responsibilities and it will be difficult to hold them accountable for results. As part of the change roles, do not forget the importance of assigning someone to coach upper management on change as it relates to software. As you saw in Chapter 8, "Government Case: Large Defense Project Behind Schedule and Over Budget," senior management needs such help because they rarely understand software.

- Look for the obvious and the low-hanging fruit as your first order of business. As you saw in Chapter 2, "Industrial Case: Organizational Change in a Large Information Technology Shop," you can use these relatively easy targets to build momentum for change. However, recognize that many technologies do not get adopted for the wrong reasons. As you saw in Chapter 9, "Government Case: Introducing New Technology," inertia, politics, personalities, and the resistance to trying something new often get in the way.

- Most barriers to change are psychological and behavioral. As you saw in Chapter 3, "Industrial Case: Justifying a Process Improvement Program for a Large Bank," these barriers are often formidable because they force people to take positions that they are reluctant to change, for no other reason than stubbornness.

- Even when you think the need for change is obvious, resistance to it can pop up from the most unexpected sources. As you saw in Chapter 6, "Industrial Case: Utility Moving to the Clouds," there were blistering attacks launched on cloud computing because the changes threatened jobs, power, and existing empires.

- Always tie change to business objectives. Then, as you did in Chapter 4, "Industrial Case: Moving to Commercial Off-the-Shelf and Open-Source Software Usage in Telecommunications," when presenting justifications for the change, let the numbers do the talking.[1]

- Not all change is good, and sometimes it makes sense not to pursue it. As you saw in Chapter 5, "Industrial Case: Small Defense Project Needs Help," sometimes the outcomes do not always happen as anticipated. In this case, the move to a cost-type contract for a Small Business Innovation Research (SBIR) program effort was catastrophic.

- Do not lose sight of marketplace discriminators when making changes. As you saw in Chapter 7, "Industrial Case: Adoption of Agile Methods," a software firm's push to adopt Agile methods failed to consider quality as the changeover was under way. The firm had to refocus its change effort because quality was something its clients really valued.

- Control the controllables, and do the things that you can do. As you saw in Chapter 8, it does not pay to waste your time and get frustrated fighting for things you really have no influence over. Focus on getting things done instead, and your effort will pay dividends.

- Do not forget that you need to expend the effort to make a product out of the technology. As you saw in Chapter 10, clients may not readily adopt the technology if user and field support are not offered.

There are many other secrets I wanted to share with you. But I have found that you can easily lose focus by sharing more than ten takeaway lessons. As a successful consultant, I learned long ago that offering too much advice can be just as bad as providing too little. Therefore, I culled my list of secrets and ranked them by importance before I shared these with you.

Lessons-learned summary

I will supplement my secrets by providing you with my Dirty Dozen lessons learned, which are derived from the case studies. These lessons are summarized in Table 12-2 with some implementation guidance. I used the following three criteria to rank these lessons by importance to limit the number offered to the dozen that I decided to share with you:

- **Bang for the Buck**   Financial return for your investment, in time and dollars, when trying to capitalize on this lesson.

- **Ease of Implementation**   The relative ease with which you can use this lesson to help facilitate and/or implement needed change.

- **Pain/Benefit Ratio** The amount of effort and frustration involved in making the change versus the benefit derived. Please note that the amount of pain involved in extracting benefits might be so large that you reject an otherwise worthy change project.

TABLE 12-2 The Dirty Dozen lessons learned when dealing with change (listed in order of importance).

Number	Lesson Learned
1	*When identifying issues that impact cost, productivity, and quality, dig deep to identify both the issues and root causes.*
	Implementation Guidance In addition to pinpointing the underlying causes using "root cause analysis,"[2] look at your performance data, metrics, and performance indicators. When put into context, these will help you understand what to do to adequately address the issues.
2	*Use industry benchmarks from reputable sources to establish cost, productivity, and quality baselines for comparison and justification of changes.*
	Implementation Guidance I would select one of the many such benchmarks[3,4] that are currently on the market that can be used to serve this function.
3	*Improvements will always take longer than expected. The reason for this is simple. Motivating change is hard and breaking down barriers takes time.*
	Implementation Guidance Assume that it will take double the time you estimate to address barriers and you will be safe most of the time.
4	*Use actual results whenever possible to gain momentum to get change adopted for widespread use. While skeptics might not believe the numbers, presenting them provides powerful evidence that the change is worthwhile.*
	Implementation Guidance If you do not have performance data, take the time to gather it. Doing so is worth the effort because it is hard to refute it. Make sure that you take the time to define your measures and validate your results thoroughly. When change is afoot, people will spend time analyzing what you present, especially if they want to challenge your conclusions in front of the bosses.
5	*To win the battles of the budget, it is important to come to the fight armed with a business justification for your expenditure, an idea for where you will find the money, and a plan for achieving the desired results.*
	Implementation Guidance Developing a compelling business case always provides a worthwhile reason for adopting change. Besides my book on the topic,[1] a business case for open-source software serves as an example.[5]
6	*There may be hidden issues that influence decisions relative to change. In Chapter 6, aging equipment and reliability issues did not surface until late in the process when options were being compared. Yet, these issues were the major drivers that governed which option was selected.*
	Implementation Guidance Try to write down all of the variables that influence change early in the change process. Often, you will be able to identify many of the hidden issues just by writing the factors that are forcing functions for the change down. Soliciting input from all stakeholders is also highly advisable to understand the issues.
7	*Those who foster change need to anticipate the perceived threats and develop plans to address them as part of their efforts.*
	Implementation Guidance The best way to address perceived as well as actual threats to change is head on. Again, first write the threats down. Then brainstorm and develop ideas on how to deal with them.

Number	Lesson Learned
8	*Getting people to deliver what they promise often takes patience, effort, and diligence. Many will do a good job. Others will let you down.*
	Implementation Guidance Use project management techniques[6] compatible with your processes and development paradigms to manage rather than monitor progress. Pay attention to the details. Believe the data rather than the people because it is rarely wrong.
9	*What works in the small does not always work in the large. This fact cautions us to be careful when you try to scale techniques that work in a laboratory to businesses at large.*
	Implementation Guidance Technology Readiness Levels have some merit for this lesson because they can be used to establish a framework by which you can assess whether a technology is ready or not to see prime time.
10	*Do not forget to keep management and stakeholders apprised of your progress and issues. Without current information, management support can seemingly waiver overnight even when you have high-level champions for change in your corner.*
	Implementation Guidance I always schedule a meeting with my bosses on a monthly basis during both good times and bad. If you leave scheduling the meeting up to them, they will call you in only when there are problems. But surprises can be eliminated and you can keep them in your corner if you take the initiative to meet with them during both good times and bad throughout the course of a change initiative.
11	*Partnering with potential users is a good idea, especially when it requires all parties to make commitments of time, staff, and money to the cause.*
	Implementation Guidance In-kind investments of equipment, facilities, and staff are just as valuable as cash contributions. The key is getting partners to ante up to show you their commitment. Have them back up their talk with some sort of investment.
12	*Understand the work that needs to be performed before developing plans to handle it. As you peel the onion, you may be surprised to find tasks that you did not have any idea that you were expected to perform.*
	Implementation Guidance I almost always recommend using a Work Breakdown Structure (WBS) to identify the activities and tasks I need to perform. Once I get this completed, I look at resources required to complete them. If resource issues occur, I ask management which of these tasks I should not perform. Often, this causes them to rethink their budget allocations and they find funds somewhere to cover the shortfalls.

Ten tools and techniques to rely on

During my discussions of the secrets of success and lessons learned, I identified several tools and techniques that I felt were very useful in putting the principles and practices to work as changes were being made. Use of the tools and techniques listed in Table 12-3 should not surprise you. Most represent implementations that good project managers from any discipline use normally during the course of their practice. However, I think it still is important to identify and encourage their skilled use to increase your chances of success as part of a change-implementation life cycle, which consists of startup, implementation, and assessment phases.

TABLE 12-3 Ten tools and techniques to rely on and how they help.

Number	Technique	How It Helps
Startup Phase		
1	Work Breakdown Structure (WBS)	Planning tool used to identify the work that needs to be performed in order to be successful in terms of tasks.
2	Critical path analysis	Technique used to find the shortest path through a schedule. Delays along this path cause proportionate delays in delivery.
3	Benchmarks	A tool used for comparing current cost, productivity, and/or quality performance to some credible reference point.
4	Root cause analysis	Technique used to pinpoint the actual, not perceived, causes of an issue. Use of actual performance data to accomplish this is highly recommended.
5	Ishikawa or fishbone diagrams[7]	A pictorial tool used to represent causes and effects. These are frequently used by the Six Sigma[8] community.
Implementation Phase		
6	Rate of progress charts	Control tool that illustrates the rate of progress you are making relative to the planned cost and schedule performance.
7	Gantt charts	Another control tool used to check the status of schedules and to show what milestones have been achieved and what events have taken place.
8	Risk matrix	A spreadsheet that identifies the top risks in terms of their impacts and how you plan to mitigate them.
Assessment Phase		
9	Project retrospective[9]	A project post-mortem conducted to identify what you did right, what you did wrong, and what you would do differently.
10	Defect measures	Tools that provide you with indicators of product quality.

What senior management wants to see

As you can glean from the tables, much of the advice I have offered focuses on getting, earning, and maintaining senior management support for the improvement engagement. Without such support, you do not stand a chance as the battles rage around you for power, resources, and attention. The three things senior management can provide you are permissions, encouragement, and shelter. Permissions are important because they provide you with the ability to start up. With permission, you can hire people, claim resources, and spend money. Encouragement is also important because it makes you believe that change is possible. However, acting as a buffer between you and others is the most important thing management can do, because it allows you to concentrate on the job rather than on the many distractions that impede your ability to get it done.

Acquiring desired senior management support is often not as difficult as you might first imagine. Most members of senior management want to leave their mark and make a difference. They just do not know either what to do or how to do it when it comes to software. The reason for this as I explained in the case studies is that most senior managers in companies engaged in commerce come from disciplines other than software. For example, they tend to have a financial background when the firm is growing and seeking investors or a legal background if the firm is in the midst of acquisitions and mergers. The trick in getting support is to make your idea the vision of the senior manager and to convince him or her that you can succeed so that the idea can triumph.

However, you need to do the following four things to gain senior management's trust when working in a situation involving organizational change:

- **Do your homework**   Gather the facts about why the change is needed and what benefits the firm can expect to reap. Also, identify who is involved and what their positions are. Identify resources that you can tap and why they are better spent on your and the manager's idea. Do some tutoring about software and the risks involved, if needed. But never talk down to them because the senior manager will resent it, even if he or she is clueless about software.

- **Talk and act like a business person**   Always talk about the business goals and the implications of the change proposal. Yes, there is a technical case that can be made for most change. But this is not what the senior manager wants to hear. Senior managers want to hear that you have command of the business situation and that the money and effort you are requesting on their part will be both earned and well spent. Remember, most firms are in business to make a profit. Focusing on how you can help achieve that should be your primary motivation.

- **Shoot straight**   Be honest, and describe the situation like it is. Answer the questions posed as best you can. Remember, "I do not know" is an unacceptable answer. Replace that with "I will find out and get back to you." Be honest with senior management about the operational setting and dynamics. Realize that you are being tested each time the senior manager asks a question or asks for information. If you pass the test, you will be trusted, and that is what you are after.

- **Deliver what you promise**   When the smoke clears, the only thing that is left is the mark you made. Senior managers will judge you based on how big this mark is and whether you delivered what you promised or not. Of course, if you keep them apprised of your progress as advised, expectations can be recast and you still can be successful. But nothing solidifies trust and confidence more quickly than someone who delivers as promised.

What workers want to hear

You also have to make sure you have the support of the masses. Without it, change will not happen. There are two dozen ways workers can sabotage a change initiative. The easiest way is for them to wait it out. Say yes, and then do nothing until forced to. That is the reason you have to build support from those affected by the change. If they back you, good things will happen. Throughout the book, I have sprinkled hints on how to build support and gain momentum for change. As a change agent, I have seen initiatives flounder for the most absurd reasons. For example, a COTS package was not made a candidate because the vendor was not green enough.

When I think about how to get the workers' support, I think of a number of strategies. Each of these works under selective circumstances. The six strategies that seem to work best are these:

- **Build alliances with project managers** The power brokers in most organizations are the project managers. They control the resources and, therefore, the destiny of the firm. Get their support by providing them with added value, and they will provide you opportunities not available through other means. Use your metrics and data to solidify their support.

- **Influence the influence-makers** In most organizations, 20 percent of the staff is responsible for 80 percent of the productivity. The opinions of those who excel in such a manner count because these people are held in high regard by everyone on the staff. Getting them to endorse your technical change initiative makes it acceptable for others to follow suit.

- **Mix it with middle managers** Make it your practice to work one-on-one with middle managers who control resources within the organization. This allows them to ask the questions they cannot ask in public. It also facilitates an information exchange and the building of a trust relationship that often leads to their support.

- **Be satisfied with a 90 percent solution** Those facilitating change need to know when good is good enough. While I am a perfectionist at heart, I realize that a 90 percent solution is sufficient in most organizations. The reasons for this are simple. Such an improvement represents a significant leap forward. The other reason is that extracting the additional ten percent of the benefit can often take a disproportionate amount of resources.

- **Deliver something that you can brag about** Deliver something meaningful and visible. Ward off criticism from those who are jealous and trying to steal your resources by producing something tangible early in the initiative. Generate a working prototype or a functional product you can show off and be proud of. Such pride will often create a groundswell of support, especially if management and opinion leaders are in your camp.

- **Be perceived as important and successful** Create an aura of success by making and celebrating a string of small successes. This will enable you to build momentum and keep rolling as you blaze to the finish line with meaningful results. Being perceived as successful is what matters because nobody wants to support an unsuccessful initiative.

Remember, you will not succeed by forcing people to adopt change. They will band together and rebel against such tactics. The way to get them to change is by motivating them to accept and adopt it. Also, remember that what motivates workers is often different than what appeals to management. Workers respond to interesting work and using cool and innovative technology, while managers are more interested in ways to achieve their business objectives.

Summary

Obviously, I believe that you can be successful with change. However, to achieve success, you have to stay focused on the things that count and try to avoid the many obstacles that can get in the way. The critical issues that pop up in all my cases are those dealing with people. That is not surprising because in most situations you are addressing organizational change. While people matter a great deal, you also need to create the atmosphere, environment, and infrastructure to help them accept and adopt new ways of doing business. Again, this is the reason why I broke down my cases into organization, project, process, product, and people segments. In order for your effort to succeed, all of these segments matter and all must be addressed as part of your change process. I hope you learned from the cases and were able to take away concepts, principles, and techniques that will facilitate your efforts at change for the better in the future. If you are able to accomplish this, my book will have served its purpose and been a success.

References

References cited within this chapter include the following:

[1] Donald J. Reifer, *Making the Software Business Case: Improvement by the Numbers* (Addison-Wesley, 2002).

[2] Duke Okes, *Root Cause Analysis: The Core of Problem Solving and Corrective Action* (American Society for Quality (ASQ) Quality Press, 2009).

[3] International Software Benchmarking Standards Group (ISBSG) published both development and maintenance benchmarks. See *www.isbsg.org* for more information.

[4] Several firms that market cost models—such as Galorath Inc. and Quantitative Software Management (QSM), Inc.—provide benchmarks as part of their product lines. See *www.galorath.com* and *www.qsm.com* for more information.

[5] Carolyn A. Kenwood, *A Business Case Study of Open Source Software,* The MITRE Corporation, Report No. MP 01B0000048, July 2001, available at the following URL: *http://www.mitre.org/work/tech_papers/tech_papers_01/kenwood_software/kenwood_software.pdf.*

[6] Harold Kerzner, *Project Management: A Systems Approach to Planning, Scheduling and Controlling,* 10th ed. (John Wiley & Sons, 2009).

[7] Kevin Kelleher, *Cause-and-Effect Diagrams: Plain and Simple* (Joiner/Oriel Inc., 1995).

[8] Warren Brussee, *All About Six Sigma: The Easy Way to Get Started* (McGraw-Hill, 2005).

[9] Norman L. Kerth, *Project Retrospectives: A Handbook for Team Reviews* (Dorset House, 2001).

Web resources

Applicable web resources that amplify points made throughout this book have been identified in each chapter. My goal is to help you by putting additional resources on my website in the future. For example, I plan to prepare an instructors guide that contains discussion questions for use in college and university classes once the book is published. As another example, I plan to add pointers to articles of interest to the community as I find them.

Please visit *www.reifer.com* and look on the home page for these links. I am hopeful that you will find these additional resources helpful.

Acronyms

The following acronyms are used within the book:

ASQ   American Society for Quality

ATM   automated teller machine

B&CS   Business & Customer Services

CEO   chief executive officer

CIO   chief information officer

CM   configuration management

CMMI   Capability Maturity Model Integration

CONOPS   Concept of Operations

COTS   commercial off-the-shelf

CPFF   Cost Plus Fixed Fee

CRM   Customer Relationship Management

CVE   Common Vulnerabilities and Exposures

CWE   Common Weaknesses Enumeration

D&B   Dunn & Bradstreet

DACS   Data & Analysis Center for Software

DCAA   Defense Contracts Audit Agency

DCMA   Defense Contract Management Agency

DOD   Department of Defense

ERP   Enterprise Resource Planning

F&A   Finance & Accounting

FP   function points

G&A   General and Administrative

GAO   U.S. Government Accountability Office

GFE   Government Furnished Equipment

GFI   Government Furnished Information

GNC   Guidance, Navigation, and Control

GPS   Global Positioning System

GUI   graphical user interface

HRM   Human Resources Management

HTML   Hyper Text Markup Language

HUD   Heads-Up Display

IBM   International Business Machines

IEEE   Institute of Electrical and Electronics Engineers

IFPUG   International Function Point Users Group

IS   Infrastructure Services

ISBSG   International Software Benchmarking Standards Group

ISO   International Organization for Standardization

IT   Information Technology

IT&E   Independent Test and Evaluation

ITG   independent test group

IV&V   Independent Verification and Validation

JPL   Jet Propulsion Laboratory

LLC   Limited Liability Corporation

MBA   Masters of Business Administration

MIT   Massachusetts Institute of Technology

NASA   National Aeronautics & Space Administration

NSF   National Science Foundation

NYU   New York University

OCC   Open Cloud Consortium

OSI   Open Source Initiative

P&L Profit & Loss

PM program manager

QA quality assurance

QSM Quantitative Software Management, Inc.

R&D Research and Development

RFI Request for Information

RFP Request for Proposal

ROI return on investment

RUP Rational Unified Process

SBA Small Business Administration

SBIR Small Business Innovation Research program

SCAMPI Standard CMMI Appraisal Method for Process Improvement

SCEA Society of Cost Estimating and Analysis

SCIFs Secure Compartmented Information Facilities

SCM software configuration management

SEI Software Engineering Institute

SIL System Integration Laboratory

SIT Stevens Institute of Technology

SLOC source lines of code

SQA Software Quality Assurance

T&E Test and Evaluation

TCO total cost of ownership

TRA Technology Readiness Assessment

TRL Technology Readiness Level

TSP Team Software Process

UAV unmanned aerial vehicle

USC University of Southern California

WBS Work Breakdown Structure

Glossary

The following definitions, many of which are unique, are offered for terms that are used within the book:

A

acquisition The process of acquiring something via a contract.

Agile software development A group of software development methodologies based on iterative and incremental development, where requirements and solutions evolve through collaboration between self-organizing, cross-functional teams.

appraisal The process of assessing the worth, significance, or status of something of interest.

architecture The structure of components, their interrelationships, and the principles and guidelines governing their design and evolution over time.

asset Something of value that a firm owns and can capitalize.

audit An independent examination of a work product or set of work products to assess compliance with specifications, standards, contractual agreements, or other criteria.

B

baseline A specification or product that has been reviewed and agreed upon, and thereafter serves as the basis for further development, and that can be changed only through formal change control procedures.

benchmark A standard against which measurements or comparisons can be made.

best practice Engineering or management activity that directly addresses the purpose of a particular process and contributes to the creation of its output (for example, metrics provide insight using measurement data to create their results). Best practices in this context are activities that are established, based on general consensus, as the most effective means of delivering such output.

budget The resources (money, people, equipment, facilities, or other assets) allocated to accomplish authorized work.

build An operational version of software that incorporates a specified subset of the capabilities that the final product will provide.

business case Materials prepared for decision makers to show them that the business idea under consideration is a good one and that the numbers make financial, as well as technical, sense for the organization.

C

Capability Maturity Model (CMM) A description of the stages through which organizations evolve as they define, implement, measure, control, and improve their software development and maintenance processes. The model provides a guide for selecting process improvement strategies and priorities by facilitating the determination of current process capabilities and the identification of the issues most critical to quality and process improvement.

Capability Maturity Model Integration (CMMI) A process improvement approach that provides organizations with the essential elements of effective processes that can be used to ultimately improve their performance. It helps integrate traditionally separate organizational functions, set process improvement goals and priorities, provide guidance for quality processes, and establish a point of reference for appraising current processes. CMMI can be used to define and improve integrated processes in an organization using diverse engineering disciplines like systems engineering, software development, and integrated product teams.

champion A high-level member of the senior management team who supports and acts as a proponent for change within the organization.

change agent The person who facilitates change in an organization.

change management The process of controlling organizational changes in a controlled manner, enabling approved changes with minimum disruption.

change model A particular way of addressing a particular category of change. A change model defines specific predefined steps that will be carried out for this category of change.

change process The set of steps, or process, used to accomplish change.

cloud computing A form of Internet-based computing, whereby shared resources, software, and information are provided to computers and other devices on demand, like either a time-share system or the electricity grid.

commercial off-the-shelf (COTS) Hardware and software products that are ready-made and available for sale to the general public on either a purchase or license basis. COTS products are used as-is, with perhaps some tailoring via parameterization and data entry. The major advantages of COTS are that it is available immediately with known level of quality at an affordable and reasonable cost.

competency Skills, knowledge, and personal attributes that enable effective work performance.

compliance Ensuring that a standard or set of guidelines is followed, or that proper, consistent accounting or other such practices are being employed.

configuration management A discipline applying technical and administrative direction and surveillance to identify and document the functional and physical characteristics of a configuration item, control changes to those characteristics, record and report change processing and the implementation status, and verify compliance with specified requirements.

contingency In management, refers to the amount of design margin, time, or money used as a safety factor to accommodate future growth or uncertainty.

contract An agreement between two or more competent parties in which an offer is made and accepted, and each party benefits. The agreement can be formal, informal, written, oral, or just plain understood. Some contracts are required to be in writing in order to be enforced.

contract terms and conditions Legal, financial, administrative, and other pertinent terms and conditions that are included as part of a contract.

core service Information Technology (IT) services that deliver basic outcomes desired by one or more customers.

cost The resources (dollars, staff, staff-hours, and other assets) required to develop an item, complete a task or activity, and/or deliver a product.

critical success factor Refers to the characteristics, conditions, or variables that have a direct influence on customers' satisfaction with the products and services that a firm offers.

culture A set of values that is shared by a group, including expectations about how people involved should behave, ideas, beliefs, and practices.

customer The individual or organization in charge of acquiring new releases for the user during the software maintenance portion of the life cycle. This person or organization may or may not be the sponsor. However, the customer will represent the sponsor and the user while managing the delivery budgets, schedules, and pressures.

D

defect The difference between a computed, observed, or measured value or condition and the true, specified, or theoretically correct value or conditions discovered via reviews by analysis (for example, a defect found via code reading during a code walkthrough).

deliverable A product, release, or increment developed, tested, packaged, and provided to satisfy customer-documented needs and/or requirements.

depreciation A measure of the reduction in value of an asset over its life. This measure is based on the wearing out, consumption, or other reduction in the useful economic value.

E

earned value A measure of budgetary performance that is used to map actual expenditures against technical achievements. This measure is often determined by milestone completions.

effectiveness A measure of the extent to which plans are realized and results are achieved.

efficiency The relationship between the resources used and the results achieved.

effort The amount of work required to finish an activity or task expressed in staff-months or staff-hours of labor.

estimate The most knowledgeable forecast of the resources (money, people, equipment, facilities, and other assets) needed in the future to complete a maintenance task.

F

framework A semi-completed software system designed to be used to generate or create a new instance of itself from a template.

function points A standard measure of software size and complexity as seen by the end user and determined from a specification by counting the number of unique inputs, outputs, inquiries, interfaces, and logical internal files.

G

governance The rules and process for ensuring that policies and strategy are actually implemented, and that required processes are correctly followed. Governance includes defining roles and responsibilities, measuring and reporting work progress, and taking actions to resolve any issues that impede its timely completion.

I

information technology A broad category of products and services that are based on digital technologies used for the creation, storage, and use of information. Computer hardware, software, communications media and content, and telecommunications equipment and services are manifestations of information technology.

infrastructure The underlying framework of an organization or system—including organizational structures, policies, standards, training, facilities, and tools—that supports its ongoing performance.

intellectual property The intangible output of the rational thought process that has some intellectual or informational value and is normally protected via using copyrights, patents, and/or trade secrets.

K

knowledge management The process responsible for gathering, analyzing, storing, and sharing knowledge and information in an organization.

L

life cycle The various stages that a software product goes through during its lifetime (that is, from product conception through retirement).

M

maturity level A well-defined, evolutionary plateau that is reached as the organization moves toward achieving a mature process.

measures Variables that are quantified to provide insight into a project or organization's information needs.

metric A quantitative measure of the degree to which a software system, process, or component possesses a given attribute. Error density, for example, provides an indicator of software reliability.

middleware The layer of software that sits between the operating system and applications that provides computing services through a single programming interface.

O

offshore Provision of services from a location outside of where the customers are based.

opportunity cost The revenue that would have been generated by using the resources in a different manner.

overhead Costs for services that cannot be allocated in full to a specific customer. For example, the costs associated with providing shared configuration-management services.

P

paradigm A modeling approach used for the software development and maintenance process (for example, waterfall, incremental development, and other approaches).

platform The hardware/software configuration on which the application runs (such as PC/Windows, Mainframe/POSIX, and other combinations).

process A sequence of steps performed for a given purpose (for example, the software repair process).

process maturity The extent to which a process is explicitly documented, managed, measured, controlled, and continually improved.

product Software and all of its associated work products (including configuration index, readme files, documentation, and other items) that represent the current configuration of the operational baseline.

project An organized undertaking that uses human and physical resources in an effort to achieve a specific goal.

project management A form of organization in which all of the people on the project report to the project manager.

Q

quality assurance A set of activities conducted to provide adequate confidence that the adopted software processes are being used and the product generated conforms to established technical requirements. In the commercial world, quality assurance sometimes refers to testers and testing.

R

risk In financial circles, refers to the exposure to loss.

risk management The process of identifying, analyzing, quantifying, and developing plans to eliminate or mitigate risk before it harms a project.

S

schedule The actual calendar time budgeted for accomplishing goals established for activities or tasks associated with a development or maintenance action.

security The protection of information so that unauthorized persons cannot read or modify it and unauthorized persons are denied access to it.

Service Level Agreement (SLA) A part of a service contract in which the level of service is formally defined. In practice, the term SLA is sometimes used to refer to the contracted delivery time (of the service) or level of performance.

service-oriented architecture An architecture that provides its users with a loosely integrated suite of services (such as authentication, database, and so forth). Underlying and enabling all of the orchestration involved is metadata defined in sufficient detail to describe not only the characteristics of these services, but also the data that drives them.

software life cycle The period of time that begins when a software product is conceived and ends when the product is retired from use. The operations and maintenance portion of the life cycle commences after delivery to the user and ends when the product is retired from use.

software maintenance According to IEEE 1219-98, it's the process of modifying a software system or its components after delivery to correct faults, improve performance or other attributes, or adapt to a changed environment.

software reliability The probability of achieving failure-free operation of software for a specified period of time in a specified environment.

software requirements The number of functional, performance, and/or interface requirements established for a release, typically in either a specification or in the applicable software change requests.

software size A measure of the amount of the software in a software system. Frequently used measures include function points, feature points, and source lines of code.

source lines of code (SLOC) The logical size of the software measured in nonblank, noncomment equivalent source lines of code. Equivalent SLOC represents a normalized measure of the equivalent new source lines of code that will be generated during the maintenance cycle.

sponsor An individual or organization acting as a proponent for change and for providing the resources for accomplishing it per the agreed-upon schedule and budget.

staff The people in an organization assigned to do the work.

staffing Management activities conducted to acquire, develop, and retain staff in an organization.

stakeholder An individual or organization with a vested interest in the maintenance of the product and who collaborates with others to identify requirements, prioritize repairs, and increase the product's fitness for use.

subject matter expert (SME) An individual who is recognized as an expert in a particular area or topic.

supplier Third parties who contribute directly to the success of an organization or project. They include, but are not limited to, contractors, subcontractors, vendors, and independent contractors and consultants who supply services on a time and materials basis.

T

technology transfer The process used to prove, transfer, and put technology into widespread use within an organization.

transition The process employed to transfer the software and the responsibility for its maintenance and support from the developer to the maintainer.

turnover The point in the life cycle when the software and the responsibility for its maintenance and support is transferred from the developer to the maintainer. For this transfer to occur, all terms and conditions spelled out in the transfer agreement must be satisfied (or waived).

U

uncertainty In management, refers to the degree of entropy associated with the information used to make decisions.

user An individual or group of individuals who use the software operationally in the field.

user support The process of providing user support, including training via mentoring, staffing a help desk, and providing a website.

V

validation The process of evaluating software to determine whether or not it satisfies specified requirements.

verification The process of evaluating software as it is developed to determine whether or not it satisfies the conditions imposed on it at the start of each phase of development.

W

work package Specification of the work to be accomplished in completing a function, activity, or task. A work package defines the work product(s), the staffing needs, the expected duration, the resources planned to be used, the acceptance criteria, the responsible individual(s), and any special considerations for the work.

work product An artifact (such as a document, code, or other item) associated with the execution of a practice.

Recommended Readings, References, and Resources

The following readings, references, and resources are provided in addition to those at the end of each chapter in the book.

Recommended Readings

While there are many books and articles on change management, the following general readings—some of which are software specific—are recommended because they contain useful guidance and are worthwhile reads:

- Eric Abrahamson, *Change Without Pain: How Managers Can Overcome Initiative Overload, Organizational Chaos, and Employee Burnout* (Harvard Business School Press, 2003).

  This is an interesting book on change that suggests that companies should alternate major change initiatives with smaller, more paced periods of change, which he calls *tinkering* and *kludging*. To reinforce his message, he presents lots of good examples from firms like General Electric, IBM, and American Express Travel.

- Gerard Blokdijk, *Change Management 100 Success Secrets: The Complete Guide to Process, Tools, Software and Training in Organizational Change Management* (Emereo Publishing, 2008).

  If you are going to read only one or two books on the topic, this should be one of them. The book provides 100 success secrets you can put to work as you introduce change within your organization.

- Esther Cameron and Mike Green, *Making Sense of Change Management: A Complete Guide to the Models, Tools and Techniques of Organizational Change*, 2nd ed. (Kogan Page, 2009).

  This volume focuses on explaining why and how change happens organizationally. In the process, it provides valuable insights into commonly used change frameworks and models.

- Thomas (Tupper) F. Cawsey and Gene Deszca, *Toolkit for Organizational Change* (Sage Publications, Inc., 2007).

  This textbook for advanced students provides useful information on available tools for those contemplating change. It also provides insights into how to measure the impacts of change, both positive and negative, on the organization.

- Michael Drafke, *The Human Side of Organizations*, 10th ed. (Prentice-Hall, 2008).

  This book looks at how job design impacts work-related behaviors within organizations. This topic is important to those initiating change, especially when behavioral aspects impact whether or not they will be successful.

- Rita Chao Hadden, *Leading Culture Change in Your Software Organization: Delivering Results Early* (Management Concepts, 2003).

  This book guides you through the change process and instructs you on how to achieve quick wins and usable results by focusing on culture change within your organization. It addresses the many social and psychological drivers and leadership traits that you must effectively manage to achieve successful outcomes.

- John Hayes, *The Theory and Practice of Change Management*, 3rd ed. (Palgrave MacMillan, 2010).

  This comprehensive textbook provides the reader with a basic understanding of the theory and practice of change management. I especially like the case studies and real-world exercises used to arm students with knowledge of how to facilitate change in practice.

- Chip Heath and Dan Heath, *Switch: How to Change Things When Change Is Hard* (Crown Business, 2010).

- Detlev J. Hoch, Cyriac R. Roeding, Gert Purkert, and Sandro K. Lindner, *Secrets of Software Success: Management Insights from 100 Software Firms Around the World* (Harvard Business School Press, 2000).

  This is one of my favorite books on change management. It provides a comprehensive and realistic assessment of what the important issues are when addressing change in most firms.

- John P. Kotter, *Leading Change* (Harvard Business Press, 1996).

  This clear and concise book on change propagates an eight-step framework for fostering change within organizations. This is another of my favorite books on the topic because it concentrates on providing examples of how to implement its recommendations in practice.

- *Managing Change and Transition* (Harvard Business Press, 2003).

  This book provides an easy-to-read guide to managing change. I recommend it because the volume provides seven practical strategies to help facilitate change in most organizations.

- Geoffrey A. Moore, *Crossing the Chasm: Marketing and Selling Technology Products to Mainstream Customers* (HarperBusiness, 2000).

  This book is another "must read." The reason I recommend this book so highly is that it focuses on what to change, why to change, and how to make change happen from a marketing point of view.

- Kate Nelson and Stacy Aaron, *The Change Management Pocket Guide and CD Bundle* (Change Guides LLC, 2005).

  This little book provides lots of useful advice on making change happen. Besides process, the book focuses on roles and how to address pockets of resistance. It is well written and a nice addition to the library of anyone who is dealing with change.

- Richard T. Pascale and Jerry Sternin, "Your Company's Secret Change Agents," *Harvard Business Review*, Vol. 83, No. 5, May 2005, pp. 72-81.

  This is an insightful article on how to facilitate change via influence-makers within your organization. It tells you how to identify and put these key change agents to work as you roll out your change initiative.

- Fran Rees, *How to Lead Work Teams: Facilitation Skills*, 2nd ed. (Jossey-Bass/Pfeiffer, 2001).

  This last recommended reading focuses on the facilitation skills needed to build consensus and put it to work as part of your change initiative. It discusses how to build and lead the teams that are an essential ingredient to making change successful in most organizations.

References

The following general change management references are offered because they help establish a disciplined framework for managing change within organizations:

- A listing of change management frameworks and models authored by the faculty at DePaul University is available at *http://facweb.cs.depaul.edu/nsutcliffe/450-00Current/450Frameworks-Models.htm*.

- ADKAR is a model for change management from the Change Management Learning Center that is explained at *http://www.change-management.com/tutorial-adkar-overview.htm*.

- The McKinsey 7S framework is useful when an alignment perspective is needed. It is described at *http://www.mindtools.com/pages/article/newSTR_91.htm*.

- SCORE is a free service that provides business mentoring and advice for those contemplating and making changes organizationally. Its services are described at *http://www.score.org*.

Other Resources

The following helpful resources are provided to help readers succeed when pursuing change within academic, industrial, and government organizations:

- Change Management Learning Center—Best Practices in Change Management 2009, available at *http://www.change-management.com/best-practices-report.htm*

- Harvard Business Review, available at *http://hbr.org*

- Massachusetts Institute of Technology/Sloan School of Management at *http://mitsloan.mit.edu*

- University College London—Change Management Toolkit at *http://www.ucl.ac.uk/hr/osd/resources/change.php*

- Wharton Center for Leadership and Change Management at *http://leadership.wharton.upenn.edu/welcome/index.shtml*

Index

About the Author

 DONALD J. REIFER is one of the leading figures in the field of systems/software engineering and management, with over 40 years of progressive experience. He has built businesses, steered troubled projects, and served in executive positions in industry and government. He specializes in the area of metrics and measurement. Besides being a trusted advisor to major corporations and the government, he has founded software businesses and served as an expert witness.

From 1993 to 1995, Mr. Reifer managed the DoD Software Initiatives Office under an Intergovernmental Personnel Act assignment with the Defense Information Systems Agency (DISA). As part of this Senior Executive Service (Three Star Equivalent) assignment, he also served as the Director of the DoD Software Reuse Initiative and Chief of the Ada Joint Program Office and worked for the Office of the Assistant Secretary of Defense (ASD/C3I), who served as the CIO for the Department of Defense.

Previously, while with TRW Inc., Mr. Reifer served as Deputy Program Manager for their Global Positioning System (GPS) efforts. While with the Aerospace Corporation, Mr. Reifer managed all of the software efforts related to the Space Transportation System (Space Shuttle). Mr. Reifer started his software career at Hughes Aircraft Company as a software engineer on the Phoenix missile project.

Currently, as President of Reifer Consultants, Mr. Reifer supports executives in many Fortune 500 firms who are developing investment strategies aimed at improving their systems and software engineering capabilities and capacity. Mr. Reifer also serves as the Principal Investigator on the firm's information warfare and software protection Small Business Innovation Research program (SBIR) efforts. For the past three years, he has been leading an Army study looking at ways to improve weapons system maintenance and sustaining engineering support. He also serves as a Visiting Associate at the Center for Systems and Software Engineering at the University of Southern California (USC) where he is involved in the COCOMO project.

Mr. Reifer was awarded the Secretary of Defense's Medal for Outstanding Public Service in 1995 for the innovations he brought to the DoD during his assignment. Some of his many other honors include the AIAA Software Engineering Award, Hughes Aircraft Company Fellowship, the Frieman Award for advancing the field of parametrics (cost estimation), and membership in Who's Who in the West. Reifer is a senior member of the ACM and IEEE and a member of INCOSE and ISPA.

What do you think of this book?

We want to hear from you!

To participate in a brief online survey, please visit:

microsoft.com/learning/booksurvey

Tell us how well this book meets your needs—what works effectively, and what we can do better. Your feedback will help us continually improve our books and learning resources for you.

Thank you in advance for your input!